vegan

on the
cheap

vegan

Great Recipes and
Simple Strategies that
Save You Time and Money

on the cheap

ROBIN ROBERTSON

WILEY

John Wiley & Sons, Inc.

Published by John Wiley & Sons, Inc., Hoboken, New Jersey

Published simultaneously in Canada

For general information on our other products and services or for technical support, please contact our Customer Care Department within the United States at (800) 762–2974, outside the United States at (317) 572–3993 or fax (317) 572–4002.

Wiley also publishes its books in a variety of electronic formats. Some content that appears in print may not be available in electronic books. For more information about Wiley products, visit our web site at www.wiley.com.

Library of Congress Cataloging-in-Publication Data

Robertson, Robin (Robin G.)
   Vegan on the cheap : great recipes and simple strategies that save you time and money / Robin Robertson.
      p.   cm.
   Includes index.
   ISBN 978-0-470-47224-8 (pbk.)
   1. Vegan cookery. 2. Quick and easy cookery. 3. Low budget cookery. I. Title.
   TX837.R6252   2010
   2009015988

Printed in the United States of America

10 9 8 7 6 5 4 3 2 1

Dedicated to the memory of my mother,

Elizabeth Gennaro

Acknowledgments

For their enthusiasm and helpful feedback, I want to thank my recipe testers who have been so generous with their time in the development of this book. A big thanks goes to Tami Noyes, Jenna Patton, Russell Patton, Tina Matlock, Cassandra Greenwald, Andrea Weaver, Melanie Baker, Lea Jacobson, Lisa Dahlmeier, Toni Dalhmeier, Chessa Hickox, Linda Evans, Becca Bennett, Lori Beth Way, Jennifer Lynsky, Melissa Chapman, Gina Rothwell, Jacqueline Bodnar, Amy Hutchings, Kathryn Bourn, Eileen Young, Caroline Morrow, Candace Burnham, and Cara Donley.

A very special thank-you to my husband, Jon Robertson, for his ongoing support and encouragement, as well as for his help in compiling the cost breakdowns for the recipes.

I am also grateful to my agent, Stacey Glick of Dystel & Goderich Literary Management, and the staff at John Wiley & Sons, especially my editor, Linda Ingroia, as well as Cecily McAndrews for editorial support and Amy Zarkos, the production editor.

Contents

Introduction

I was born into a family of thrifty cooks. My Italian grandmother, for example, never wasted even the tiniest scrap of food. A favorite family legend relates how she once saved three leftover peas rather than throw them out—no doubt, they ended up in the next day's soup.

My mother, in turn, learned many thrifty recipes from my grandmother, and regularly created feasts for our family of four out of very little, from a simple and delicious cabbage and bread soup to the weekly pot of pasta fazool. With a heritage like that, I've come by my cooking "on the cheap" consciousness naturally.

These days, most of us are on an ever-tightening budget. With skyrocketing food prices, even buying the basics has our grocery bills reaching new highs. A steady stream of newspaper and magazine articles and other media reports suggest many ways to save money on food, and interestingly, "eat more vegetarian meals" is one of the primary suggestions.

Those of us who enjoy a plant-based diet already know that saving money on the food bill is just one of many benefits of eating vegan. Still, within the broad range of people currently eating a plant-based diet, some eat more economically than others. The reason is that some of us cook using a lot of whole grains, beans, and seasonal produce. Others rely on prepared foods and specialty items to make up their weekly menus, which are exponentially more expensive.

The fact is, when time is short, many vegans and other health-conscious people have difficulty striking that golden balance between their hectic schedules and eating healthy while trying to cut down on the cost.

Enter *Vegan on the Cheap*, a cookbook that I wrote for people who want to prepare easy and delicious vegan meals as economically as possible. *Vegan on the Cheap* brims with quick, creative, and satisfying recipes that save time and money. It's designed to show you how to manage your kitchen time as well as your grocery bills to make quality, inexpensive meals in a fraction of the time. Best of all, the book guides you on ways to be as frugal as you want to be with easy-to-follow strategies. You can incorporate as many of the strategies as you wish to fit your schedule and lifestyle. This is the first vegan cookbook to focus on the economy of both time and money—all with delicious, nutritious recipes that will be a pleasure to serve your family.

Since getting dinner on the table quickly often means using expensive convenience foods, *Vegan on the Cheap* provides you with creative cost-saving strategies, such as making your *own* convenience foods and meat alternatives. This way you'll save both money and time, while eating great meals in the process. For example, vegans who enjoy seitan know the prepared versions can be expensive. In this book, you will discover the secret of making great seitan yourself in minutes and at a fraction of the cost. The same goes for other popular prepared products—such as vegan mayonnaise, veggie burgers, and peanut sauce. These products are great because they save time, but they can be expensive. *Vegan on the Cheap* will show how you can make them yourself easily and economically.

The truth is now out about animal-based diets—they can lead to poor health, they can be expensive, and they can damage the environment. So it should be easy to think of the 150 recipes in *Vegan on the Cheap* as not only kind to our pocketbooks and good for us, but as kind to the environment as well, making this the ultimate "green" cookbook.

Among the recipe chapters in *Vegan on the Cheap* is Soup and Stew Savvy, which includes hearty stews and soups such as Black-and-White Bean Chili (page 78) and Southern New Year's Stew (page 76) that are meals in and of themselves. There is also a chapter entitled Noodle Know-How, a collection of satisfying and economical pasta and noodle dishes from East to West, featuring recipes such as Dan Dan–Style Linguine (page 124) and Fusilli with Potatoes, Green Beans, and Lemon Basil Crème (page 119). Other chapters contain recipes for great skillet combos using grains and beans, main-dish salads, and dollar-stretching casseroles. You will also find a dessert chapter filled with sweet delights that taste anything but frugal.

As food prices continue to soar and the number of vegans continues to rise, there has never been a better time for *Vegan on the Cheap*. In addition to enjoying the great-tasting economical recipes within these pages you will also discover a number of helpful strategies and tips such as how to:

- Avoid processed ingredients

- Make your own meat alternatives at a fraction of the cost of commercial products

- Save time with menu planning, grocery shopping, and meal preparation

- Freeze a stockpile of prepared ingredients for the weeks ahead with the "Big Batch" concept

- Enjoy one-pot cleanup and a day off cooking with "Two-for-One Meals"

- "Splurge a Little" with simple additions and substitutions

- Figure out your food budgets with costs-per-servings, with no recipe costing more than $2 per serving

Whether you're trying to maximize a dwindling food budget or just trying to be a thrifty cook, let *Vegan on the Cheap* be your practical guide to help save your money while you enjoy delicious, inexpensive, and healthful meatless and dairy-free meals.

The Big Picture

*T*he advantages are many when you choose a vegan diet, from the health benefits to helping animals to the "green" effect a vegan diet has on the environment. There are also economical advantages, since a plant-based diet generally costs less than a meat-centered one. But these days, even basics like rice, wheat, and fresh produce are more expensive, so the cost of eating vegan has risen as well. This is especially true if you consider the pricey convenience foods that many of us with busy schedules have come to rely on.

Across the board, as food prices soar and packages shrink, more of us are tightening our food budget belts. To some people, this means simply going out to restaurants a few less times a month. At the other end of the spectrum, it can mean planting your own vegetable garden and baking your own bread. The majority of us may fall somewhere in between, looking for ways to prepare healthful, well-balanced, and economical meals at home.

For many of us, convenience foods may be the first things to go when attempting to lower the cost of our weekly grocery bill. But then there's the time factor: With hectic lives, it can be difficult to budget our time in the interest of saving money. That's where this book can help, as it provides strategies and recipes designed to save both time and money.

How a Vegan Diet
Can Save You Money

1. Grocery bills. Plant-based products tend to be less expensive than animal products. For example, basic plant proteins, such as beans, cost less than $1 a pound and tofu around $2 per pound. Even certain "convenience foods," such as frozen veggie burgers and frozen veggie burger crumbles, can cost less than $1 per serving.

2. Medical bills. Eating a well-balanced plant-based diet can go a long way toward boosting the immune system. As a result, you may find that you have fewer colds or that they don't last as long. Additionally, a diet based on animal products has been shown to be a leading cause of heart disease and some cancers; thus, a plant-based diet could save you money on future medical bills.

3. Dining out. Vegan options in restaurants are usually less costly than meat and seafood options. You may also find yourself dining in ethnic restaurants such as Thai, Indian, and Chinese, where prices are generally less expensive than traditional American restaurants. If you live in a rural area like I do, where the only vegan food available is the bean burrito (hold the cheese) at Taco Bell, you'll save money on dining out simply because there's nowhere to go! We eat at home most of the time and save lots of money in the process.

Tips for Saving
Money and Time

Following is a list of meal planning, grocery shopping, and food preparation strategies that can save you time or money or both. Some are simple techniques that you may be using already. Others may take a little more effort on your part. Read them over and decide what's best for you and your lifestyle. If you give some of them a try, you'll find that even small changes can yield big results in saving time and money. I've been using most of them for years.

1. Meal Planning Tips

-   Strategy Session. Set aside fifteen minutes once a week to develop a menu for the week and make a shopping list. I do mine on Sunday afternoon.

- **Planned Leftovers.** Plan one or two meals a week that you can stretch into two meals each. It can be as simple as making extra rice on Sunday to turn into a fried rice dish on Tuesday or making extra pasta on Saturday to enjoy in a stir-fry on Monday. It can also mean making a seitan pot roast for Sunday dinner and having enough left over to sauté the next night with mushrooms and lemon juice or a red wine sauce. Perhaps you've also included enough potatoes and other vegetables in your pot roast to work into a new side dish, making a new meal with the addition of some roasted Brussels sprouts. If you make a large casserole or pot of stew, consider all that you can do with the leftovers. They can be used for lunches, served again for another dinner, or portioned and frozen for easy single-serving future meals.

- **A Matter of Taste.** Just because it's thrifty doesn't mean it can't taste fabulous. It's important to cook what you and your family enjoy eating. Even the cheapest dish won't save you a nickel if nobody likes it. Rotate recipes to eliminate repetition and utilize spices, herbs, and other seasonings to enhance the flavors of basic ingredients.

- **Stick to Staples.** Let many of your meals revolve around pantry staples such as rice and beans or pasta. (It's likely that some of these are family favorites as well!) Come up with different ways you enjoy making these staples and keep that list handy. Between family favorites (see below) and staple-based meals, you should have at least twenty-four regular meals from which to choose.

- **Incorporate Family Favorites.** Make a list of your family's favorite dishes. Try to come up with at least a dozen choices, allowing each family member to include a favorite. Chances are good that many items on the list will already be thrifty, such as veggie chili, pasta with marinara sauce, pizza, burritos, or noodles with peanut sauce. Include several of these dishes in your weekly menu, and rotate them each week, adding one or two new items. Plan all your meals for the week ahead of time, allowing for one or two nights of leftovers. Use your menu plan to make your grocery shopping list.

- **Be a Thrifty Cook.** Cut down on waste in other ways, too. For example, save vegetable trimmings to make a vegetable stock or turn broccoli stalks into a slaw. Use older bread in bread puddings or stratas or to make croutons or bread crumbs. Add water to jars of sauces and shake them to get the last spoonful. Before juicing lemons or limes, bring them to room temperature and roll them on the countertop with the palm of your hand to get more juice.

- Include More Soups and Stews. What's more soothing than a bowl of soup or stew? Their virtues are many, from being easy and versatile to make to being adaptable and forgiving, not to mention that they are the ultimate dollar-stretcher. Whenever your fridge gets low, check around and see if you can't get one more meal out of what's left before going to the store. If you have even one onion and two carrots on hand, then a pot of soup can't be far behind. If you have a piece of celery, too, then it's a sure bet. Chop them up, add water or stock from your freezer, simmer them a bit, add some seasonings, and then look around for what else you have. A potato? Some frozen vegetables, such as limas or spinach? How about a can of diced tomatoes and a can of beans? Do you have a bit of leftover rice or pasta? Soon, a pot of soup is ready for the tasting.

- Jazz Up Rice and Beans. Get creative with rice and bean combos, and you'll always have something great cooking. While some omnivores may still be skeptical, savvy vegans know that bean and grain dishes don't have to be austere fare. As the Moroccan-Inspired Lentil Soup (page 201), Southern New Year's Stew (page 76), Rice Island Casserole (page 170), and other recipes in this book show, beans and grains can mean haute cuisine with the right seasonings. From the Bean and Barley Salad with Creamy Dijon Dressing (page 90) to the Black Bean Soup with Kale and Rice (page 200), grain and bean combinations run the gamut from soups and sautés to salads and pilafs. Best of all, they're inexpensive, easy to make, and delicious.

- Keep Your Kitchen Well Stocked. To help make a feast out of simple ingredients, keep your pantry stocked with a variety of non-perishables such as canned tomatoes, canned beans, and pastas, as well as grains, nuts, and seasonings. Keep frozen veggies on hand for those times when you run out of fresh veggies, as this will save a trip to the store.

- Pantry-Raid Recipes. Keep a few easy pantry-based recipes handy (on the fridge or in a kitchen drawer or taped inside the pantry door) to remind you of simple easy meals that you enjoy and can put together quickly. This will save last-minute panics when you're starved and don't know what to cook. If you have a box of pasta and a can of beans in the pantry, you're within twenty minutes of a satisfying meal that can save you from the expense of dialing for takeout.

Some of my favorites include: Ziti with Green Olives, White Beans, and Oven-Dried Tomatoes (page 113), Radiatore with Escarole and White Beans (page 112), and Almost-Instant Chickpea-Tomato Soup (page 63).

- Déjà Stew. An easy and satisfying way to save on your food budget is to create an entirely new meal out of a few leftovers. If on any given day my refrigerator holds a container of leftover rice, pasta, or potatoes, it's sure to be featured in the dinner menu that night. When

Déjà Stew

Since most of the ingredients are already cooked, this stew comes together quickly, but tastes as rich as if it simmered for hours. If you have leftover gravy from your pot roast, add it to enrich the stew, replacing some of the broth, if desired. To stretch the stew even further, add some cooked pasta or rice near serving time. You can also add a cup or two of cooked vegetables or beans if you have some on hand or substitute them for any ingredients in the stew that you may not have in the fridge, such as seitan. **Makes 4 servings**

1 tablespoon olive oil
1 large yellow onion, chopped
1 cup vegetable stock (page 45)
½ teaspoon dried thyme
½ teaspoon dried savory
2 cups diced seitan (from Slow-Cooker Seitan Pot Roast, page 213)
3 cooked potatoes, diced (from Slow-Cooker Seitan Pot Roast, page 213)
2 cups cooked sliced carrots (from Slow-Cooker Seitan Pot Roast, page 213)
1 (14.5-ounce) can diced tomatoes, drained
1 cup frozen peas, thawed

1. In a large pot, heat the oil over medium heat. Add the onion, cover, and cook until softened, about 10 minutes. Add the broth, thyme, and savory.

2. Add the seitan, potatoes, carrots, tomatoes, and peas, stirring gently to combine. Simmer for 10 minutes. Taste and adjust the seasonings, if necessary. Serve hot.

I have seitan, potatoes, and carrots left over from a pot roast, I transform them into a wonderful stew and feel as though I've struck gold.

2. Grocery Shopping Tips

- **Make a Grocery List.** Anyone who shops for vegan groceries in a supermarket knows there are several departments that can be avoided entirely. Still, it can be helpful to have a grocery list template, organized by department, such as Fresh Produce, Canned Goods, Frozen Foods, and Grains and Pasta, and you can fill in what items you need in the appropriate category. If you find that you purchase basically the same ingredients each week, it may be easier to have a master grocery list on which you simply highlight the items you need before you go shopping.

- **Shop Once Per Week.** Decide on a day and time to do your shopping that fits your schedule but that also coincides with a time when the store is less crowded. If you can limit your shopping trips to once per week, it can save time and gas, as well as the money you might spend from impulse shopping when running in for "just a few things."

- **Shop Seasonally.** Buy in-season produce grown in your area. Locally grown produce at the peak of its season is usually cheaper both at the farmer's market and the supermarket. I don't need to tell you that fresh, locally grown produce also generally has better flavor.

- **Grocery Shopping No-Brainers.** Take advantage of specials; avoid impulse purchases; don't shop when you're hungry; use coupons; buy generic store brands.

- **Shop for Store Sales and Stock Up.** Stock up on frozen and canned foods when they're on sale. Save money with on-sale produce, but avoid waste by buying only what you can use right away or freeze for later use. I always stock up when my store has a sale on nonperishables I use all the time, such as canned beans or tomatoes. In general, keep your pantry and freezer well stocked with good-quality ingredients for quick and easy meals.

- **Buy in Bulk, Within Reason.** Many localities have wholesale warehouse "clubs" where you can buy anything from groceries and toiletries to computers and televisions. Some areas have wholesale "cash and carry" grocery stores that cater to restaurants but are open to the public. While I've found some great deals at these stores for specific items, for the most part it isn't a practical option for just two people with limited storage space. Check out one in your area and decide if it makes sense for you.

- Shop Ethnic. Check out the ethnic grocery stores in your area for low-cost produce, rice, and other items. I actually found roasted peeled chestnuts in an Asian market for ninety-nine cents in a vacuum-sealed bag that were selling in the supermarket for $9 a jar!

- Support Community Agriculture. Whether you join a CSA (Community Supported Agriculture) group, where you pay a fee and receive fresh produce each week throughout the growing season, or simply shop at your local farmer's markets, the food should prove to be less expensive than supermarket produce. It should also taste better and have more nutrition because it's fresher and it hasn't been shipped across the country and stored in warehouses. Determining if this is a practical and money-saving choice for you may depend on the number of people in your family and the amount of produce you are required to buy (some CSAs allow for half shares) as well as the distance you would need to drive to pick up your produce. Do your homework to find out what is available in your location. Begin by visiting the Web site of Local Harvest (www.localharvest.org/csa) for a list of CSA farms in your area and to find out more about how it works.

- Produce Stands and Pick-Your-Own Farms. If you don't have a CSA or farmer's market in your area, scour the classifieds in your local paper for produce stands and pick-your-own farms. You'll find that there are small vegetable stands nearby or out by the road in front of local farms. The pick-your-own farms and orchards are usually less expensive and can be a fun way to get some outdoor exercise.

- Don't "Go Organic" into the Poorhouse. While true organic produce is best, it's also more expensive. If you really need to tighten the belt, buy organic only when you can get it at a reasonable price. Then don't feel guilty if some of the produce you buy isn't organic; just be sure to wash all your produce well, peel anything that isn't organic, and be glad you're able to eat fresh food and still save some cash. Eating lots of vegetables is ultimately more important than whether or not those vegetables are organic.

- Grow Your Own. Even if you don't have a large yard, if you have even the smallest porch, patio, balcony, or windowsill, you can probably grow a few vegetables and you can definitely grow some herbs. Fresh herbs are superior in flavor, but expensive—so grow your own if you can.

- Go for Frozen. Think frozen, especially during the winter months when fresh produce prices are through the roof. Frozen vegetables have been found to be more nutritious than much of the fresh supermarket produce that has been shipped many miles and spent a long time in warehouses. Frozen vegetables are generally less expensive than fresh, and they can save time as well since they're already cleaned and cut. Here are some frozen favorites that I keep on hand:

  - Peas

  - Spinach

  - Corn kernels

  - Brussels sprouts

  - Cut green beans

  - Lima beans

  - Sliced tricolor bell peppers (when I run out of the ones I grew and froze in the summer. Both are infinitely cheaper than a fresh red or yellow bell pepper in winter.)

- Postpone Your Grocery Shopping. See how long you can postpone your weekly shopping trip by using up what you have on hand in the refrigerator, freezer, and pantry. You may be pleasantly surprised by what you'll find. I do this frequently and am sometimes actually able to go nearly a week beyond my normal shopping day, cutting my total grocery budget for the month significantly. The added benefit of doing this is that it encourages you to rotate items in your larder—frozen foods that are approaching their "use by" date and nonperishables that have been pantry fixtures for quite some time—as well as use up stray produce that might otherwise go bad. Another benefit is that it stimulates your creativity. I like to choose a few items from my stash and put them on the counter, then let my imagination take over as I think about how to combine them. For example, a can of white beans, crushed tomatoes, garlic, and a box of pasta have "yummy dinner" written all over it. Some quinoa, walnuts, a bag of frozen peas, and a single onion can make a fine pilaf. And so on.

- Use Store Cards. Even if you're not a coupon clipper, you can save lots of money by signing up for your local store savings card. Just by letting them swipe my card when checking out at the supermarket, I save an average of $15 a week on my grocery bill. Just recently, I got a five-pound bag each of potatoes and onions for free, a dollar off a pound of grapes, and much more. Depending on the weekly promotions, it can add up to a lot of savings.

3. Food Preparation Tips

- Big-Batch Cooking. Once a week, prepare large amounts of a few basic foods, then portion and freeze them for later use. Choose items that can be used throughout the week or portioned and frozen such as a big pot of brown rice, beans, pasta sauce, or vegetable stock (see chapter 2).

- Make Your Own. You might also make a dessert, quick bread, or seitan (a wheat-based protein that can cost nearly $5 for an eight-ounce package in a store but can be made at home for a little over a dollar per pound).

- One-Pot Meals. Once a week, make a big one-pot meal that can stretch to two nights—a hearty soup or stew, chili, casserole, or slow-cooker meal.

- Two-for-One Freezer Meals. Make double amounts of specific meals such as stews, chili, casseroles, and burgers, and freeze half. This strategy has the added benefit of the "one-pot cleanup," to cut down on dish-washing time and energy.

- The Vegetable Chop. When it's time to chop an onion for soup, chop an extra one and also make chili or stew. If you need to wash two celery ribs for a recipe, take the time to wash the whole bunch and cover and refrigerate the rest until you need it. Peel and mince an entire head of garlic at a time, so it's ready when needed. Store it covered in olive oil in a jar with a tight-fitting lid. Wash and spin-dry your lettuce as soon as you get it home—it will last longer. If veggies are cut, cleaned, and ready to use, we save time when cooking. It also encourages us to use and eat more vegetables. Carrot and celery sticks, for example, can be stored in zip-top bags in the vegetable bin for up to a week for you to enjoy as a healthy snack or to chop into your next soup or stew. Tightly covered chopped onions will keep refrigerated for up to three days, or frozen for 3 to 4 weeks. The same is true for bell peppers.

- Advance Prep Times Two. Double (or even triple) recipes for frequently used dressings and sauces, then refrigerate or freeze the extra to become handy homemade convenience foods. By using this strategy once a month, you can get dinners on the table in a flash without relying on expensive commercially packaged products.

- Save Electricity. Double up in the oven—when you bake potatoes, make extra to use later in the week. Rely on your slow cooker, pressure cooker, and rice cooker to save on energy costs.

- Be a Creative Cook. Maximize ingredients. The easiest example of this is to use vegetable scraps to make stock. Or use leftovers to make another meal. Or my favorite, list ways to use leftover mashed or baked potatoes, then try one idea each week. Here's a start. Use extra cooked spuds to make: shepherd's pie, potato pancakes, samosas, stuffed dosas, mac and cheese sauce, pierogis, potato bread, potato muffins, and so on.

- Cook Favorite Takeout and Restaurant Food at Home. Perhaps the most important way to save money on food is to cook at home more and eat out less. Again, this is something that only you and your checkbook balance can decide. But let's take a hypothetical: If you used to go out to eat once a week and have decided to cut back to once a month, then you may find yourself going through

Freeze It, Don't Waste It

Recipes often call for a small amount of an ingredient that is available only in larger amounts, such as canned chipotle chiles, tomato paste, or coconut milk. Rather than put the leftovers in the refrigerator in the hopes of using them up within a few days, it's best to freeze what you don't use to be sure it doesn't go to waste. In the case of an ingredient such as tomato paste, you can measure it out in 1-tablespoon scoops and freeze them on a baking sheet, since recipes usually call for it by the tablespoon. Once frozen, place all the little lumps of tomato paste in a freezer bag and you'll have it ready (and measured) when you need it.

Fresh herbs, especially fragile ones such as parsley, basil, and cilantro, need extra care, too. If there's a chance you won't use your herbs within a few days, puree what you don't need with a little oil and freeze in small containers to use later to enrich sauces, soups, and stews.

"restaurant withdrawal." One helpful solution is to make eating in fun by duplicating some of your favorites, whether it's Bean and Cheezee Rice Burritos (page 187) or Chinese takeout such as the Better-Than-Takeout Tofu Stir-Fry (page 142).

- Make Your Own Convenience Foods. From salad dressings to seitan, there are a number of ways to save money when you start making your own convenience items. The next chapter is filled with such recipes, including Vegetable Stock (page 45), Make-Your-Own Mayo (page 41), and Big Stick Pepperoni (page 56).

- Brown-Bag It. For years I packed a lunch for my husband to take to work, while his coworkers either went to restaurants or bought expensive offerings from the lunch delivery service. Most often, his lunch would consist of leftovers from dinner the night before. We estimate that he saved a couple thousand dollars a year just by doing this, and he enjoyed his homemade lunch every day.

- Dessert on a Budget. Dessert doesn't have to be expensive to be delicious. Pricey ingredients such as nuts, chocolate, vegan cream cheese, and natural sweeteners can add up when combined to make delicious vegan confections. One way to compromise is to use a limited amount of the more expensive ingredients so you have a "taste" of the good life without breaking the bank. For example, use toasted nuts or chocolate to garnish a dessert. Stretch a pint of vegan ice cream, which is notoriously expensive, by turning it into an ice cream cake with peanut butter, chocolate, or fruit. Make bread puddings and rice puddings—inexpensive to make, yet they taste great, make a lot of servings, and are better for you than some other desserts.

- Make Your Kitchen a "No-Waste Zone." One way to save money in the kitchen is to cut down on waste. We already talked about saving vegetable scraps and odd bits of veggies for stock, but what about leftover cooked veggies from dinner or a few stray berries, or a single apple that never seems to get eaten? If you keep passing them over, they'll eventually reach the point of no return, and you'll have to toss them. That's like putting cash in the trash. Instead, be diligent in using them up as soon as you can. Add leftover cooked veggies to salads or put them in the bottom of your soup bowls and pour servings of hot soup over them (the soup will heat them). If you can't convince someone in your family to simply eat whatever fruit happens to be languishing on the counter, then incorporate it into dinner. A sliced apple or pear makes a great addition to a green salad or slaw. Or you can combine your pear or apple with other wallflower fruits, such as those grapes and berries or that last banana, for example, and you will have a nice fruit salad for dessert. If there's not enough to stretch, add a small can of pineapple and some dried cranberries.

- Cook Ethnic. Since much of the world's population has long been eating frugally by necessity, many nations have a rich menu of tasty and economical fare. When you cook the "peasant food" of a particular cuisine, you're offering your family exotic flavors and great nutrition while also saving money. My mother frequently prepared Italian *povero* dishes such as Pasta e Fagioli (page 64) and Mom's Bread and Cabbage Soup (page 65) that were so good, it never occurred to me that we were on a tight budget.

Time Is Money: Striking a Balance

In looking for ways to save money on your food bill, there is a tradeoff in the time it can take to prepare less costly items. Most of us can't do it all, so it's important to choose the things that jump out at you and say, "Now *this* is something we use a lot, and if I can make it myself, I can save a bunch." For example, if you don't eat much bread or don't like seitan, then you won't be tempted to use the cost-saving tips regarding those items. However, if you eat a lot of soups and salads, then the homemade stock and salad dressing recipes may be right up your alley. Of course, the "batch cooking" idea (page 9) in this book is something that could be helpful to anyone, regardless of what you prepare.

As for "growing your own"—if you have a long commute for work and lots of extra activities, tending a vegetable garden may be out of the question. Some people, however, may find that converting a small patch of backyard crabgrass into delicious produce not only saves money on food, but also the bending, stretching, and "sweat equity" involved in gardening may actually eliminate gym fees.

Dining Out

When money is tight, going out to eat may seem like a luxury you can't afford. Still, there may be times when you want to get out of the house or must eat out because of traveling and so on. Here are some tips for dining out economically.

Dressing Up and Cheaping Out

- Search for specials such as prix fixe menu deals, before-theater menus, and early-bird specials

- Look for restaurants that offer two-for-one entrées

- All-you-can eat salad bars are always a bargain

- Go out just for drinks and appetizers

- Skip the drinks—have them at home

- Go out for lunch instead of dinner

- Share an entrée

- After dinner out, have dessert and coffee at home

- Have dessert out and dinner in

Restaurant Night at Your House

If going out for dinner on Saturday nights is not within your budget, why not have "restaurant night" at home with your partner, friend, or family? Plan a menu that includes restaurant favorites or some other special meal. Set your table with a tablecloth and candles. Serve the meal plated on the "good" china, arranging the food aesthetically with a flourish. Garnish your plates like works of art, even if it's just to add a sprig of parsley. Serve the meal in courses. Play dinner music to match the mood and the food. Linger over coffee and dessert and bask in the glow of how much money you saved.

No Skimping Allowed

There are some ingredients that you simply shouldn't cheap out on. They are high-quality ingredients for which a cheaper alternative is either unpalatable or unavailable. Here are the top ones on my list:

Extra-virgin olive oil. Most supermarkets carry decent enough store brands of extra-virgin olive oil. Just don't settle for anything less than "extra-virgin" on the label.

Pure maple syrup. Never use "pancake" syrup—there is no comparison to the flavor and goodness of pure maple syrup.

Pure vanilla extract. Don't even consider buying imitation vanilla extract. Pure vanilla extract is worth every penny (and you only use a tiny amount at a time, anyway). If you happen to find vanilla beans at a bargain price, they're worth buying. They keep well and are superior in flavor to even pure extract.

Nuts. Nuts are a wonderful source of protein and other nutrients and are infinitely versatile. They can be expensive, but if you think of them as an important ingredient and not just a snack food, you'll see them in a new light. Most of the recipes in this book that include nuts call for small amounts of cashews, walnuts, or almonds, three of the most practical, nutritious, and economical nuts that can be used in anything from sauces and main dishes to salads and desserts.

To bring out the flavor of raw nuts, toast them for a short time before using.

To toast nuts in the oven: Preheat the oven to 350°F. Arrange nuts on a baking sheet and toast until golden brown and fragrant, 5 to 10 minutes depending on the variety, stirring occasionally. Watch closely so they don't burn. Set aside to cool.

On the stovetop: This is best for small amounts of nuts or for seeds. Spread the nuts or seeds in a single layer in a dry skillet over medium heat. Toast them, shaking the pan and stirring until they are golden brown and fragrant, 5 to 7 minutes, depending on the variety. Remove immediately from the skillet so they don't continue to cook. Set aside to cool.

Lemons and limes. There is no comparison between fresh and bottled lemon and lime juice. Buy only the amount of citrus you need so there's no waste. If a recipe doesn't call for the zest, zest the fruit anyway and freeze it if not needed right away. The zest can be used to enliven pilafs, muffins, bean purees, and sauces, among other things. Bring your citrus to room temperature before juicing to get more yield.

Imported black olives. You should be able to find jars of reasonably priced kalamata olives in your supermarket or discount store. These are far superior to supermarket canned black olives, which taste like the can they came in. Good olives have such a rich flavor that you don't have to use a lot in a recipe to benefit from them. Look for ethnic markets that have olive bars for another good source at a reasonable price.

Nutritional yeast. Unparalleled for adding its cheesy-salty flavor to vegan dishes, nutritional yeast is an excellent source of protein and B-complex vitamins, including B_{12}. Not to be confused with brewer's yeast, nutritional yeast is available at natural food stores and online. Nutritional yeast is expensive, so shop around for the best price.

Herbs and spices. Spices, herbs, and other seasonings are critical to good cooking and should not be overlooked. Among the herbs that should always be used fresh are parsley, cilantro, and basil. Some dried herbs, such as thyme, oregano, dill weed, rosemary, tarragon, and marjoram, are fine in cooking when fresh are unavailable. I occasionally use dried basil in certain recipes, but fresh is always preferable. Basil is particularly easy to puree and freeze in a little oil when it's in season so you have some to get you through the winter months.

Because they can be expensive, look for spices available in bulk at natural food stores to buy only what you think you'll need for the next few months. (This is especially handy when trying out a new spice until you know you like it.) After a year, spices lose much of their potency, so if you have spices that have been around awhile, use them or lose them. Always pinch dried spices between your fingers before adding to a recipe to help release their flavor.

Eating Right
and Eating Well

This book isn't about making tomato soup out of what's left in the ketchup bottle or reusing your tea bags; it's about taking stock of your shopping, cooking, and eating habits and making adjustments wherever you feel it's needed. In addition to great time- and money-saving recipes, this book provides the questions to ask yourself—and many of the answers as well. When you prepare food from scratch, there are tradeoffs: It takes more time and effort to prepare quality home-cooked food than it does to put together a meal with expensive processed or prepared foods. Only you know for yourself how much you are able and willing to do.

Cheapskate Breakfast Ideas

Vegan breakfast is by nature relatively inexpensive, but here are some tips to make sure your breakfast is truly on the cheap.

- Sure, your mother told you this a thousand times, but I'll say it again: Don't skip breakfast. A bowl of hot oatmeal, for example, can provide energy for your day and help you avoid expensive pitfalls, such as stopping for a coffee and bagel on the way to work or school.

- Bring your own coffee, smoothie, or juice when going out to avoid spending big bucks at a coffee shop. The money you save will astonish you.

- If you're not a "breakfast person" or need something quick and easy, try a slice of toast with peanut butter or a banana smoothie. If you need something portable, bring along a peanut butter and jelly sandwich or a bag of trail mix.

- Have breakfast for dinner—serving breakfast food such as pancakes or a tofu scramble with fried potatoes and toast for dinner is both easy and economical, and it also makes a nice change from the usual dinner menus.

About the Recipes

The recipes in this book call for locally grown seasonal produce, basic pantry items, grains, beans, tofu, and tempeh, as well as homemade seitan and an arsenal of "in-house" convenience foods that you make yourself. Therefore these recipes are designed for maximum flavor and nutrition at a minimum of cost. So while you won't be seeing recipes that call for truffle oil or mai-take mushrooms, for example, you will find the occasional "Splurge a Little" notation at the bottom of some recipes. These "splurges" will offer easy ways to amp up the recipe a bit with the addition of a pricier ingredient, thus allowing for individuals to decide if they want to spend the extra money to add a fillip to a particular dish. The splurge ingredients may range from artichokes and avocados to a commercial vegan cheese.

Ingredient Substitutions

For one reason or another, whether because of a food allergy or personal preference, you may want to make an ingredient substitution in a recipe. Most of these recipes are flexible enough to allow for such changes. For example, where soy milk is called for in recipes, you can use rice milk, almond milk, or other non-dairy milk. If you have a sensitivity to gluten, then you may substitute tempeh or extra-firm tofu for the seitan in many of the recipes calling for that ingredient. Where seitan is used in small pieces, such as soups or stews, you can try your favorite bean instead. When it comes to beans, the bean varieties are interchangeable in most recipes.

Cost Consciousness

Using several recipes from the Cooking Basics chapter, the chart on the following page compares the costs of making the items yourself to buying the same quantity of the product from your supermarket or natural food store. Bear in mind that actual costs are relative and will depend on regions, brands, store sales, and other factors.

Cost Comparison Chart

Store-Bought Product	*Vegan on the Cheap* Recipe	To buy same quantity at store	Total savings over store-bought
Salsa	**Salsa in Season (page 34)**		
16-ounce jar (2 cups) = $2.89	2 cups (16 ounces) = $1.47	$2.89	$1.42
Sun-Dried Tomatoes	**Oven-Dried Tomatoes (page 33)**		
8 ounces (1 cup) = $7.49	8 ounces (1 cup) = $2.72	$7.49	$4.72
Marinara Sauce	**Marinara Sauce (page 32)**		
24-ounce jar (3 cups) = $3.59	56 ounces (7 cups) = $4.99	$8.40	$3.41
Mayonnaise	**Make-Your-Own Mayo (page 41)**		
16-ounce jar (2 cups) = $5.19	1 cup (8 ounces) = $1.65	$2.60	$0.95
Sour Cream	**Vegan Sour Cream (page 42)**		
12 ounces (1½ cups) = $2.99	2 cups (16 ounces) = $1.49	$4.00	$2.51
Salad Dressing (on average)	**House Salad Dressing (page 43)**		
8-ounce bottle (1 cup) = $3.29	1½ cups (12 ounces) = $1.49	$4.94	$2.79
Asian Peanut Sauce	**Easy Peanut Sauce (page 40)**		
8-ounce jar (1 cup) = $4.99	1½ cups (12 ounces) = $1.85	$7.49	$5.64
Chutney	**Cheapskate Chutney (page 39)**		
15-ounce jar (1¾ cups) = $6.49	2½ cups (20 ounces) = $2.62	$9.30	$6.68
Canned Beans	**A Pot of Beans (page 46)**		
15-ounce can (1½ cups) = $.80	6 cups cooked (48 ounces) = 1.69	$3.24	$1.55
Whole Grain Bread	**Three-Grain Bread (page 48)**		
24-ounce loaf = $4.79	2-pound loaf (32 ounces) = $1.57	$6.40	$4.83
Seitan	**Simple Simmered Seitan (page 50)**		
8-ounce package = $4.99	2 pounds (32 ounces) = $4.45	$19.94	$15.39
Vegan Sausage	**Close to Mom's Sausage Patties (page 54)**		
12-ounce box (patties or links) = $5.69	1 pound (16 ounces) = $2.49	$7.52	$5.03
Vegan Pepperoni	**Big Stick Pepperoni (page 56)**		
4-ounce package = $3.99	about 1 pound (16 ounces) = $2.29	$15.96	$13.67
Vegetable Broth	**Vegetable Stock (page 45)**		
1 quart (4 cups) = $3.19	6 cups = $1.50	$4.80	$3.30

Total savings over store-bought: $72.39

Five Favorite Dishes, Two Ways

Whereas the Cost Comparison Chart compares basic ingredients used in certain recipes, such as seitan, peanut sauce, and salad dressing, here are a few complete recipes of popular dishes that illustrate the cost comparison of making them using *Vegan on the Cheap* recipes versus making the same dishes using expensive store-bought ingredients.

Cheapamole (page 35) = $2.44
vs.
guacamole made with 3 avocados, $1.29 each = $5.32
Savings = $2.88

Spaghetti Marinara with Wheatballs (page 110) = $6.31
vs.
pasta made with bottled sauce and
store-bought vegan meatballs = $9.98
Savings = $3.67

Pepperoni Mushroom Pizza (page 190) = $3.52
vs.
pizza made with packaged vegan pepperoni
at $3.99 per 4 ounces = $5.89
Savings = $2.27

Cajun-Spiced Seitan Po' Boys (page 181) = $3.65
vs.
po' boys made with store-bought seitan
at $4.99 per 8 ounces = $8.62
Savings = $4.97

Build-Your-Own Fajitas (page 188) = $6.81
vs.
fajitas made with store-bought seitan, salsa, and
vegan cheese, and avocado guacamole = 15.19
Savings = $8.38

Menus on the Cheap

Below is a week's menu for a family of four using recipes in this book, followed by a shopping list. The menus illustrate how you can serve a varied menu every night of the week without breaking the bank. The average meal cost per person is around $2—each meal includes a soup or salad, main dish, and dessert.

The menu (and shopping list) could be simplified if you have an arsenal of food stashed in the freezer. For example, if you have several varieties of cooked beans and cooked rice in the freezer, you won't need to buy those items or cook them for this menu; simply defrost and use. If you have a batch of marinara sauce and some Wheatballs (page 57) in the freezer, you might prefer to use have them for dinner one night instead of one of the other meals.

Four dessert recipes are included in these menus, allowing for some of the desserts to be served two nights in a row. Or, instead of preparing dessert, you may prefer to serve fruit, vegan ice cream, or no dessert at all. The items in brackets indicate additional "go withs" to complement the meal.

Most of the recipes (except desserts) serve around four people, so if you have more people to feed, you may need to double up on some recipes or add an additional menu item, such as a salad or bread. At the same time, if there are fewer than four at your table, you can save the leftovers to enjoy as a "free lunch" the next day, refrigerate or freeze them for a future dinner, or cut out one of the menu items, if it seems like more food than you will eat.

The order of the menus has to do with grocery shopping day, which many people do on Wednesdays to take advantage of store sales. To that end, Wednesday's dinner menu is an easy one, especially if you make the Pasta Slaw (page 91) a day ahead and have Very Veggie Burgers (page 179) ready to cook. I've also arranged it so that some of the more perishable ingredients, such as lettuce, are used shortly after shopping. In my house, we use a lot of lettuce, so I usually buy a head of softer, more perishable lettuce to use up right away, and also a firmer, crisper head for later in the week. Note: If Wednesday isn't your shopping day, simply shift the days and menus accordingly.

Wednesday

Pasta Slaw (page 91)

Better Bean Burgers (page 178)

[rolls, condiments]

[cookies from previous day]

Thursday
Tossed Salad with House Salad Dressing (page 43)

Pasta e Fagioli (page 64)

Tiramisù Bread Pudding (page 238)

Friday
So Easy Vegetable Soup (page 198)

Samosa Pie (page 174)

[bread pudding from previous day]

Saturday
Tossed Salad with House Salad Dressing (page 43)

Pepperoni-Mushroom Pizza (page 190)

Apple Clafouti (page 230)

Sunday
Almost-Instant Chickpea-Tomato Soup (page 63)

Slow-Cooker Seitan Pot Roast (page 213)

Chocolate Cupcakes with Peanut Butter Frosting (page 222)

Monday
Cheapamole (page 35)

[tortilla chips]

Black and White Bean Chili (page 78)

Brown Rice (page 47)

[cupcakes from previous day]

Tuesday
Thai-Style Pineapple Rice Salad (page 97)

Mu Shu Burritos (page 148)

Gold Bar Cookies (page 218)

Grocery Shopping List

The grocery list on the following page includes all the ingredients you will need to make the recipes listed in the Menus on the Cheap (pages 20–21). Included in the list are ingredients that are probably already on hand in your pantry, such as salt, pepper, and dried spices, as well as flour, oil, and vinegar. You may already have many of the other items on hand as well, such as beans, pasta, and rice.

Average Cost of Recipes

This book emphasizes saving money without sacrificing good nutrition or great taste. To help guide you, you'll notice icons with the recipes such as "Less than (<) $2/serving" and "Less than (<) $1.50/serving."

To arrive at the average cost of the recipes in this book, I used a median price for ingredients purchased in a supermarket or natural food store. Depending on your location, the time of year, store sales, and other factors, you could probably spend less (or more) on your ingredients. In the case of spices, for example, the estimate includes just the amount of spices used, not the cost of buying entire new spice containers, since spices last for several months and most of us have a well-stocked spice cupboard.

The actual cost for making the recipes in this book can vary due to several other factors, including whether you use:

- Homemade vs. store-bought ingredients

- Premium vs. generic brand products

- Organic vs. non-organic ingredients

- On-sale or in-season items vs. items not on sale or out of season

- Homegrown or farmer's market produce vs. supermarket produce

Based on what I pay and where I live, I've found that the recipes in this book cost me less than $1.85 per serving, with more than 50 percent costing under $1.00 per serving, with an average serving cost of $.98. Here's how it breaks down:

- All of the recipes cost less than $1.85 per serving to make

- 134 recipes cost less than $1.50 per serving

- 76 recipes cost less than $1.00 per serving

- 31 recipes cost less than $.50 per serving

Grocery Shopping List

Fresh Produce:
onions
potatoes
carrots
celery
green onions
garlic
lettuce
cabbage
green bell peppers
mushrooms
small red chiles
ginger
parsley
cilantro
lemons
limes
apples

Other Perishables:
vegan margarine
soy milk or other
  non-dairy milk
tofu
frozen peas
frozen lima beans
Italian bread
burger rolls
flour tortillas
vegetable broth

Nonperishables:
penne
elbow macaroni
brown rice
jasmine rice
white beans
black beans
chickpeas
walnuts
peanuts
cashews
tortilla chips
diced tomatoes
crushed tomatoes
chipotle chiles in
  adobo
chopped green chiles
wheat gluten flour
nutritional yeast
unsweetened cocoa
  powder
apricot or peach
  preserves
golden raisins
hoisin sauce
toasted sesame oil
sherry vinegar
rice vinegar

On-Hand Pantry Items:
creamy peanut butter
old-fashioned oats
all-purpose flour
sugar
light brown sugar
confectioners' sugar
olive oil
neutral vegetable oil
  (such as canola)
apple cider vinegar
soy sauce
ketchup
instant yeast
salt
black pepper
baking powder
baking soda
pure vanilla extract
garlic powder
onion powder
paprika
ground cayenne
curry powder
ground coriander
dried basil
dried oregano
dried thyme
dried savory
crushed red pepper
ground cumin
ground cinnamon
chili powder
bay leaves
coffee

These costs may vary for you. Naturally, if you find ingredients at a cheaper price than those I used for my estimates, your results may cost less. On the other hand, if you buy higher-end items such as out-of-season produce or live in an area where food costs are higher, the recipes will cost you more.

You can use a general rule of thumb that the recipes providing the most cost savings (at around $1 per serving) are those made with beans and whole grains and less expensive vegetables such as carrots, potatoes, and cabbage. The higher-cost recipes (in the $1.85 per serving range) tend to call for ingredients such as tempeh, nuts, olives, and more expensive produce, such as fresh spinach or portobello mushrooms.

Please remember that the costs used are for illustrative purposes, but feel free to use the icons as a guide to the relative costs to help you plan your daily and weekly meals.

A Tale of Two Kales

Where I live, there is only one supermarket where although I can't always get what I want, I can always find what I need—and I usually end up saving money. Take kale, for example. My local store always has a large display of fresh kale. It's the common curly-leafed kind and it's inexpensive. For less than a dollar, I can bring home a huge bag of delicious nutrient-dense greens. There's nothing fancy about this type of kale, but it tastes great and is nutritious, and the price is right. This brings me to another variety of kale known as Tuscan black, or dinosaur kale. If I drive an hour due west, I can find this lovely heirloom variety for sale at $4 for what amounts to a small precious handful—and that's before it cooks down. I know that if I lived closer to the store with the "fancy" produce, I'd be tempted to load my cart not only with Tuscan kale, but also fingerling potatoes, wild mushrooms, heirloom tomatoes, and more. Lucky for me, I can get perfectly fine, if not gourmet, ingredients right down the street. And save a bundle in the process. My local store recently had a "buy one get one free" sale on a five-pound bag of white potatoes for $3.99—that's ten pounds. For the same amount of money, I can buy just about one pound of fingerlings! This is not sacrificing, this is smart shopping.

Cooking Basics

ooking healthful and delicious meals can be expensive, but especially so if you rely on the many high-quality convenience foods that are available. There's a point we reach where each of us must analyze the "time versus money" factor. If you can afford to invest a little time in preparing some of your own convenience ingredients, then you can save a whole lot of money.

By implementing some of the cost-saving recipes and strategies in this book in your day-to-day cooking, you will find that you not only save money, but you can actually save time, as well. Keeping a stockpile of ingredients at your fingertips can help you plan your meals and make fewer trips to the supermarket. A well-stocked refrigerator, freezer, and pantry can also enable you to get a nutritious meal on the table in minutes, thus eliminating the spontaneous "let's eat out" or "let's order takeout" because the cupboard is nearly bare when it's dinnertime.

In this chapter, you will find recipes for preparing some everyday ingredients in advance, such as rice, beans, and vegetable stock, as well as several frequently used sauces and meat alternatives that are often sold premade. Many of the convenience products available in stores come at premium prices, such as salad dressings, vegan mayonnaise, and pasta sauces. Using the recipes in this chapter, you can make them yourself at a fraction of the cost. An added benefit is that you can customize the seasonings to suit your own taste.

I've also included a recipe for tomato salsa as well as a variation on sun-dried tomatoes that are prepared in the oven (although you can also make them in a food dehydrator, if you have one). The salsa recipe comes with a caveat—while homemade salsa is great, it's only cost effective if you have inexpensive seasonal tomatoes, either those you've grown yourself or perhaps bought at a good price at a farmer's market. When tomatoes aren't in season, it's more economical to buy bottled salsa—just watch for sales and you can find a jar of good-quality salsa for about what you'd pay for two or three of those flavorless pale supermarket tomatoes.

Your Daily Bread

If you're reeling from the sticker shock of buying organic vegan bread, then think about baking your own. If you're concerned about the time involved in doing so, consider a bread machine. Until recently, I resisted buying a bread machine, thinking it was "cheating" and that I should make bread completely from scratch. The problem was that my life was so hectic, I never quite had time to bake bread, so I bought the best whole grain vegan bread I could find at my local supermarket. Even though it was expensive, it was convenient. But when the price of a store-bought loaf suddenly went from simply expensive to out-of-the question, I revisited the idea of a bread machine. Now I wish I hadn't waited so long.

For the price of about seven loaves of supermarket bread, I have a handy little machine that makes bread-making as easy as pushing a few buttons. Just pour your ingredients into the pan insert and the machine literally does the rest. It kneads and proofs for just the right amount of time and bakes it to perfection (using a fraction of the energy it would take to bake in the oven). And the machine beeps when the bread is done. Best of all, the house is filled with that heavenly aroma of fresh baked bread, and you haven't made your arms tired. My bread machine paid for itself quickly, and we now enjoy great-tasting whole grain bread, and many variations, on the cheap.

I'm not trying to convert anyone to using a bread machine, but I did want to share my own experience. If you prefer baking bread the old-fashioned way, more power to you. But if you don't have time to bake and don't want to pay a high price for good bread at the store, then this may be the answer for you, too. Bread machines come with a little booklet filled with recipes to try. Some of them aren't vegan, so you may have to experiment with veganizing them (using soy milk instead of dairy milk, or olive oil or vegan margarine instead of butter, for example). After experimenting with several combinations of ingredients, I hit upon a three-grain loaf that is my husband's favorite for his morning toast. I've included the recipe in this chapter. It has become our "daily bread" that I make each week for less than half of the cost of a loaf from the store—wait until you taste it toasted! Note: For those without a bread machine, I've also included a version of the recipe for mixing by hand and baking in a regular oven.

While it is possible to make your own tempeh and tofu at home from scratch, I think it's more practical to buy these soybean-derived ingredients ready-made, since the process to make them at home may take more time than most people can afford to spare. Further, the cost of these two protein-dense foods is actually quite reasonable.

Seitan, on the other hand, can be relatively quick and easy to make at home using wheat gluten flour, often sold as "vital wheat gluten" in most supermarkets and natural food stores. Look for it in the baking section. The cost savings of homemade seitan is staggering when compared to purchasing packaged seitan. In addition, you can use wheat gluten flour to make your own vegan sausage, cutlets, and pepperoni, too—all quite costly at the market—and you can freeze them in quantity.

While many of the recipes in this chapter can be enjoyed on their own, most of them are foundational recipes or components used in various other recipes throughout this book.

Cheap Tricks

Here is a list of some common ingredients or products and the cost-cutting alternatives you can make in your own kitchen to replace them:

Commercially Prepared Vegetable Broth (Canned or Aseptic Package)

Cheap Trick: Make your own broth—it's easy and nearly effortless (page 45). For emergencies, keep on hand a jar of good-quality concentrated vegetable base (available in paste or powder form). A container of miso paste can also be used to enrich sauces and soups. If you prefer using canned broth, dilute it by half when you use it and get more bang for your buck.

Vegan Parmesan Cheese

Cheap Trick: Like other vegan cheese alternatives, vegan Parmesan can be expensive. So what can you use to sprinkle onto pasta and casseroles to give it that salty-cheesy flavor? Make your own Faux Parm (page 38), a delicious topping made with ground nuts, nutritional yeast, and salt.

Packaged Bread Crumbs

Cheap Trick: Make your own bread crumbs—toast slices of bread evenly in a low oven until dry and lightly browned, turning once or twice. Remove from the oven and allow to cool completely, then break into a food processor and pulse until they are fine crumbs. Store in an airtight container. If using within a week, you can store them at room temperature. For longer storage, stash them in the freezer.

Bottled Salad Dressing, Sauces, and Marinades

Cheap Trick: The commercial versions are exorbitantly priced and not nearly as good as homemade. When you make your own dressings you enjoy better, additive-free flavors customized to your taste and have more money in your pocket. See House Salad Dressing (page 43), as well as recipes for other basics such as Easy Peanut Sauce (page 40), Vegan Sour Cream (page 42), and Make-Your-Own Mayo (page 41).

Creamy Mushroom Gravy

<50¢ per serving

Makes about 2½ cups

This easy all-purpose gravy is so rich and flavorful, you'll want to use it on everything, from veggie burgers to rice and beans. It's also great on seitan, grain and bean loaves, and as a binder for noodle and potato casseroles.

1 tablespoon olive oil
½ cup minced onion
2 garlic cloves, minced
1½ cups chopped white mushrooms
2 tablespoons soy sauce
1 teaspoon dried thyme
¼ teaspoon salt
¼ teaspoon black pepper

1½ cups vegetable stock (page 45)
¼ cup plain unsweetened soy milk
2 tablespoons nutritional yeast
2 tablespoons cornstarch
1 teaspoon browning sauce, such
   as Kitchen Bouquet or Gravy
   Master

❶ In a medium saucepan, heat the oil over medium heat. Add the onion, cover, and cook until softened, about 5 minutes. Add the garlic and mushrooms and cook, stirring, until softened. Stir in the soy sauce, thyme, salt, and pepper.

❷ Transfer the mushroom mixture to a high-speed blender. Add ¾ cup of the vegetable stock and blend until smooth. Add the remaining ingredients and blend until smooth.

❸ Return the mixture to the same saucepan and bring to a boil, stirring constantly. Reduce heat to low and continue stirring until the gravy is thickened, about 3 minutes. Serve hot.

Marinara Sauce

Makes about 7 cups

Commercially prepared marinara sauce is convenient, but it can be expensive. It's quick and easy to make your own for less, using crushed tomatoes. If you have a supply of homegrown tomatoes, you can, of course, use them instead.

2 tablespoons olive oil

1 medium yellow onion, finely chopped

3 garlic cloves, minced

¼ cup shredded carrot (optional)

2 tablespoons dried marjoram

1 teaspoon dried basil

2 (28-ounce) cans crushed tomatoes

1 teaspoon sugar

¾ teaspoon salt

¼ teaspoon black pepper

1 In a large saucepan, heat the oil over medium heat. Add the onion, cover, and cook until soft, about 8 minutes. Add the garlic and cook for 30 seconds. Stir in the carrot, if using, and marjoram and basil and cook until the carrot is softened, about 5 minutes. (If necessary, add a tablespoon or two of water to keep from burning.) Stir in the tomatoes and sugar and bring to a boil.

2 Reduce the heat to low, season with salt and pepper, and simmer until thickened, stirring occasionally, about 30 minutes. If not using right away, cool to room temperature and then store, tightly covered, in the refrigerator for up to 4 days. This sauce also keeps well in the freezer for several weeks.

Oven-Dried Tomatoes

Makes about 1 cup

Sun-dried tomatoes add a wonderfully rich flavor to recipes, but they can be expensive. When fresh tomatoes are at their peak, you can dry your own tomatoes in the oven. They taste great and save money, too. When your oven-dried tomatoes are gone, you can use the remaining tomato-infused oil for salads, sautés, or pasta dishes.

6 ripe Roma (plum) tomatoes, halved lengthwise

2 tablespoons olive oil, plus more to store tomatoes (optional)

Salt and black pepper

1 Preheat the oven to 225°F.

2 Place the tomatoes in a large bowl. Add the 2 tablespoons oil and season with salt and pepper to taste, tossing to coat.

3 Arrange the tomatoes on a baking sheet, cut side down. Bake until the tomatoes have shrunk to about half their original size. This should take about 5 hours.

4 Remove the tomatoes from the oven to cool for about 30 minutes. Use your hands to remove their skins. The tomatoes can be left whole and stored in a zip-top bag or chopped and placed in a jar with a tight-fitting lid. If desired, pour enough oil over the tomatoes to cover and close the lid tightly. Store the tomatoes in the refrigerator. Properly stored, the tomatoes will keep for several weeks.

Note: If you have a food dehydrator, you can use it to dry tomatoes. Just follow the instructions that came with your machine.

Salsa in Season

< 50¢
per serving

Makes about 2½ cups

Nothing beats the flavor of homemade salsa, and the savings are terrific, too, especially if you grow your own tomatoes and herbs or buy them at a farmer's market at the height of the season. Because off-season tomatoes are expensive and not very flavorful, it makes sense to buy bottled salsa during those times.

2 large ripe tomatoes, finely
   chopped
1 jalapeño, seeded and finely
   minced

¼ cup minced yellow onion
3 tablespoons chopped fresh
   cilantro, parsley, or basil
Salt

1 Combine all the ingredients in a medium bowl and mix gently to combine. Cover and set aside for 20 to 30 minutes before serving.

2 If not using right away, refrigerate until needed. The salsa tastes best if used on the same day that it's made, but will keep for up to 2 days if properly stored.

Cheapamole

< 50¢ per serving

Makes about 3 cups

Avocados are notoriously expensive, so I've been searching for a way to have my guacamole and afford it, too. After much trial and error, I've come up with this green pea and white bean dip that looks and tastes remarkably like the real deal. As a bonus to being cheaper than regular guacamole, this version also contains less fat and more protein.

2 garlic cloves, minced
1½ cups frozen peas, thawed
1 cup cooked or canned white
    beans, drained and rinsed
1 (4-ounce) can diced green chiles,
    drained
2 tablespoons fresh lime juice

1 teaspoon olive oil
1 teaspoon ground cumin
2 tablespoons minced red onion
2 tablespoons chopped
    fresh cilantro
Salt and black pepper

1 In a food processor or blender, combine the garlic, peas, beans, and chiles and blend until smooth.

2 Add the lime juice, oil, and cumin and blend until well combined. Use a rubber spatula to scrape the mixture into a medium bowl. Stir in the onion and cilantro. Season with salt and pepper to taste.

3 Cover and refrigerate for at least 30 minutes to allow flavors to blend. This tastes best if used on the same day that it is made. Use it as a dip for chips or cut vegetables or any way you would use regular guacamole.

Splurge a Little

Add mashed ripe avocado to replace a portion of the peas or white beans.

Cheezee Sauce

<$1.00 per serving

Makes about 2½ cups

This thick, flavorful sauce is drastically less expensive than commercial cheese alternatives—and it tastes better than many of them, too. Use it in casseroles such as the Tortilla Strata (page 156) or Mexican Rice and Bean Bake (page 159), as a topping for grain and vegetable dishes such as the Nacho Taco Salad (page 94), drizzled onto your favorite pizza, or anytime a cheesy flavor is in order.

⅔ cup nutritional yeast
3 tablespoons cornstarch
1¼ teaspoons salt
½ teaspoon garlic powder
2 cups plain unsweetened soy milk
   or water

1 tablespoon olive oil
2 teaspoons fresh lemon juice
2 teaspoons apple cider vinegar
1 teaspoon yellow mustard

1 In a medium saucepan, combine the yeast, cornstarch, salt, and garlic powder. Turn the heat on medium and whisk in the soy milk. Cook, stirring, until the sauce thickens, about 1 minute.

2 Remove from the heat and stir in the oil, lemon juice, vinegar, and mustard. The sauce is now ready to use. If not using right away, refrigerate the sauce in a container with a tight-fitting lid, where it will keep for several days.

Tofeta (Tofu Feta)

<50¢ per serving

Makes 4 servings

Keep this tasty tofu feta on hand to add flavor and protein to salads such as Roasted Root Vegetable Salad with French Lentils and Walnuts (page 88) and main dishes such as Orzo Pilaf with Tofu Feta (page 117).

8 ounces extra-firm tofu, drained and patted dry	2 garlic cloves, crushed
$\frac{1}{3}$ cup olive oil	1 teaspoon salt
$\frac{1}{3}$ cup fresh lemon juice	$\frac{1}{2}$ teaspoon dried oregano

❶ Cut the tofu into $\frac{1}{2}$-inch cubes and place them in a shallow bowl. Add the oil, lemon juice, garlic, salt, and oregano and toss to combine.

❷ Set aside to marinate for 30 minutes, turning once halfway through. The tofeta is now ready to remove from the marinade and use in recipes. Refrigerate any unused tofeta in the marinade in a tightly covered container. Properly stored, it will keep for 3 days.

Faux Parm

Makes about ¾ cup

For a fraction of the cost of store-bought Parmesan cheese alternative (or real Parmesan cheese, for that matter), you can whip up a batch of this tasty topping to sprinkle on your pasta and grain dishes, salads, and casseroles—anywhere you want a bit of salty-cheesy flavor.

½ cup slivered raw almonds
3 tablespoons nutritional yeast
½ teaspoon salt

In a food processor, finely grind the almonds, pulsing to avoid overprocessing. (Do not overprocess or it will turn into a paste). Transfer the almonds to a small bowl. Add the yeast and salt and stir to combine. Keep your faux parm stored tightly covered in the refrigerator, where it will keep for up to 2 weeks.

Variation

You can substitute walnuts, sesame seeds, or another nut or seed for the almonds.

Cheapskate Chutney

<50¢ per serving

Makes about 2 cups

Sweet-hot chutney is a wonderful condiment, especially with Indian meals or to jazz up rice-and-bean dishes or baked or fried tofu, tempeh, or seitan. This recipe is extremely versatile. I chose to use the combination of canned pineapple and dried fruit simply because they're always on hand and available; however, different varieties of fresh fruit may be used as well.

1 tablespoon neutral vegetable oil

¼ cup minced red onion

1 tablespoon minced hot chile or ½ teaspoon crushed red pepper

2 teaspoons grated fresh ginger

2 tablespoons light brown sugar

⅛ teaspoon salt

1 tablespoon water

1¾ cups minced canned pineapple, well drained

½ cup chopped mixed dried fruit (see Note)

2 tablespoons apple cider vinegar

In a small saucepan, heat the oil over medium heat. Add the onion and chile. Cover and cook until softened, about 3 minutes. Add the ginger, sugar, salt, water, pineapple, and dried fruit and bring to a boil. Reduce heat to low and stir in the vinegar. Simmer for 5 minutes, stirring frequently. Transfer to a bowl and cool to room temperature. Taste and adjust the seasonings, if necessary. Serve at room temperature or chilled. Store tightly covered in the refrigerator, where it will keep for up to a week.

Variation

Replace the canned pineapple with a soft fresh fruit such as chopped peaches, mangoes, or apricots. You can also replace the pineapple with a firm fresh fruit, such as apples or pears, but you will need to cook a bit longer until the fruit softens.

Note: Mixed dried fruit is sold in packages and in bulk in well-stocked supermarkets and natural food stores. It usually contains dried apricots, plums, and raisins and sometimes also includes dried apples and dates. If unavailable, use raisins (no need to chop these) alone or in combination with chopped dates, dried apricots, or other dried fruit.

Easy Peanut Sauce

Makes about 1½ cups

I adore peanut sauce for its great flavor and amazing versatility, whether using it as a dip for veggies or fried tofu or as a sauce for pasta. Why pay more for bottled peanut sauce when you can make your own on the cheap with this easy recipe?

½ cup creamy peanut butter
⅓ cup soy sauce
3 tablespoons rice vinegar
1½ tablespoons light brown sugar

2 tablespoons toasted sesame oil
2 teaspoons grated fresh ginger
½ teaspoon Asian chile paste
Water

1 In a medium bowl, combine the peanut butter, soy sauce, vinegar, and sugar. Add the oil, ginger, and chile paste and stir until smooth and well blended.

2 Taste to adjust seasonings, adding more chile paste if you prefer more heat. Add as much water as desired to reach preferred consistency. Use immediately or cover tightly and refrigerate until needed. Properly stored, this sauce will keep for several days.

Make-Your-Own Mayo

< 50¢
per serving

Makes about 1 cup

The cashews add a creamy richness to this homemade mayo. Many natural food stores sell raw cashews in bulk. Although they can be a bit costly, most recipes only call for a small amount. When they go on sale, I like to buy a couple pounds and freeze them since they're great to use in so many things, from creamy desserts and sauces to this yummy mayo.

½ cup unsalted raw cashews or
   sliced raw almonds
1 garlic clove, crushed
¼ cup plain unsweetened soy milk

2 tablespoons apple cider vinegar
½ teaspoon salt
⅛ teaspoon ground cayenne
2 tablespoons olive oil

1 In a high-speed blender, grind the cashews and garlic to a paste. Add the soy milk, vinegar, salt, and cayenne, and blend until smooth.

2 With the machine running, slowly add the oil in a thin stream until the mayo is creamy. Taste and adjust the seasonings.

3 Transfer to a small bowl or a jar, cover, and refrigerate until needed. Properly stored, it will keep in the refrigerator for 3 to 4 days.

Vegan Sour Cream

Makes about 2 cups

Commercial vegan sour cream is delicious and convenient but it can be expensive, so here's a recipe to make it yourself. Use it in any recipes calling for sour cream (such as the Seitan and Mushroom Goulash, page 208) or as a topping for baked potatoes.

1 (10.5-ounce) package firm
    silken tofu
2 tablespoons fresh lemon juice
1 tablespoon neutral vegetable oil

1 teaspoon apple cider vinegar
1 teaspoon sugar
½ teaspoon salt

Crumble the tofu into a blender or food processor. Add the remaining ingredients and process until smooth and well blended. Taste and adjust seasonings, if necessary. Transfer to a container with a tight-fitting lid and store in the refrigerator, where it will keep for several days.

House Salad Dressing

< 50¢ per serving

Makes about 1 cup

My husband, Jon, calls this basic vinaigrette, embellished with garlic and basil, our "house dressing" because it's the one I usually have on hand at our house. I prefer sherry vinegar for its richly complex flavor, but almost any kind you like will work fine.

1 garlic clove, crushed
⅔ cup olive oil
¼ cup sherry vinegar
½ teaspoon dried basil

½ teaspoon sugar
½ teaspoon salt
¼ teaspoon black pepper

1 Combine all the ingredients in a small jar with a tight-fitting lid. Shake to blend. Set aside to allow flavors to blend. The dressing tastes best if allowed to sit at room temperature for 30 minutes before using.

2 Store any unused dressing tightly covered in the refrigerator. Properly stored, it will keep for several days in the refrigerator, although the flavor of the garlic will intensify as it sits.

Variations

Even More Basic Vinaigrette: Omit the garlic and basil from the recipe above.

Soy Vinaigrette: Omit the salt and add 1 tablespoon soy sauce; use rice vinegar to replace all or part of the sherry vinegar; omit the olive oil and instead use ½ cup grapeseed oil plus 1 tablespoon toasted sesame oil; omit the garlic or include it, according to your taste.

Lemon Vinaigrette: Replace the vinegar with fresh lemon juice; omit the basil and garlic.

Mustard Vinaigrette: Add 1 teaspoon (or a bit more to taste) spicy brown mustard (or Dijon if you've got it) to the vinaigrette. Omit the basil.

Handy Hummus

Makes about 2 cups

Hummus can come in handy in a number of ways, whether used as a dip for chips or as a spread for sandwiches and wraps. It's also good as a base for a sauce or a topping for cooked vegetables, beans, grains, and pasta.

1½ cups cooked or 1 (15.5-ounce) can chickpeas, drained and rinsed

2 garlic cloves, minced

½ teaspoon salt

¼ teaspoon ground cumin

Pinch ground cayenne

⅓ cup tahini (sesame paste)

3 tablespoons fresh lemon juice

2 tablespoons olive oil

1 In a food processor, combine the chickpeas, garlic, salt, cumin, and cayenne and process until smooth. Scrape down the sides of the processor.

2 Add the tahini, lemon juice, and oil and blend until smooth. Transfer to a small bowl. If not using right away, cover tightly and refrigerate until needed. Properly stored, it will keep for 3 to 4 days.

Splurge a Little

When serving as a dip, place the hummus in a small shallow bowl and smooth the top, then drizzle with a little olive oil and spoon a few tablespoons of chopped pitted kalamata olives in the center.

Vegetable Stock

<50¢
per serving

Makes about 1 quart

A good vegetable stock has a multitude of uses, from enriching soups and stews to adding flavor to pilafs and sauces. While you can certainly make your stock with whole fresh produce, such as onions, carrots, and celery, this recipe provides ways to make it even more economical by incorporating vegetable trimmings and limp veggies. I can usually gather enough trimmings after about three days of cooking. Just make sure the trimmings you use are well washed and dried, with no sign of decay. Either way, the result will be far less expensive than buying broth at the store. Vegetables and trimmings to avoid are members of the crucifer family (cabbage, broccoli, and so on) because of their strong flavors as well as beets for their strong color.

> 6 cups chopped vegetables (onions, carrots,
>   and celery) and/or vegetable trimmings
>   (celery leaves, carrot peelings, potato
>   peelings, scallion and onion parts including
>   peel, herb stems, mushroom stems)
> Water

❶ Place the vegetables and/or trimmings in a large pot and add enough water to cover. Bring to a boil, then reduce heat to low and simmer, covered, for 1 hour.

❷ Let cool and then strain the stock, discarding the solids. The stock can be refrigerated for 2 to 3 days or frozen for about 2 months. For convenience, freeze the stock in 1- or 2-cup portions.

Variation

Slow-Cooker Method: Place your vegetables and water in a slow cooker, put on the lid, and cook on Low for 6 to 8 hours.

Note: In addition to keeping homemade stock on hand, it's a good idea to have a jar of vegetarian broth base in your cupboard to enrich soups and sauces or to make a quick stock when you don't have any. Many different brands of vegetable base are available in both paste and granular form. Better than Bouillon Vegetable Base and Vogue Veggie Base are two brands that I like.

A Pot of Beans

< 50¢
per serving

Makes about 6 cups

One pound of dried beans produces about 6 cups cooked. When cooking dried beans it makes sense to cook up a pound at a time, since they take so much time (and energy) to cook. They freeze well, so they are ideal for portioning and freezing to use as needed. This is a generic recipe—the actual cooking times will vary depending on the size and age of the beans used.

1 pound dried beans	**2 garlic cloves, crushed**
6 to 8 cups water	**1 to 2 teaspoons salt (optional)**
2 bay leaves	

1 Soak the beans overnight in enough water to cover.

2 Drain the beans and put them in a large pot with 6 to 8 cups of fresh water (older and larger beans will require more water). Cover the pot and bring to a boil. Reduce the heat to a simmer, add the bay leaves and garlic, and cook, partially covered, until the beans are tender, 1 to 3 hours, or longer, depending on the bean. (Add additional water if needed to keep the beans covered while cooking.)

3 About halfway through cooking, add the salt, if using. When the beans are tender, drain them. They are now ready to use.

Variation

Slow-Cooker Method: Cook the beans in your slow cooker to save energy and free yourself from watching the pot. Simply place the soaked beans in your slow cooker with the water, bay leaves, garlic, and salt, if using. Put on the lid and turn the cooker on Low for 8 hours.

Note: Although canned beans are relatively inexpensive and infinitely convenient, they still cost about three times as much as the same amount of cooked dried beans. If you cook a different pot of beans each week and freeze them in measured portions, you'll soon have a stockpile of beans at your fingertips that are as convenient as canned.

Rice Two Ways

Makes 6 servings

Here are two basic rice recipes, one for the stovetop and one for the oven. Both are easily doubled for batch cooking. If you want to add more flavor to the rice, cook it in vegetable stock (page 45) instead of water or add a teaspoon or two of vegetable broth base. Depending on the saltiness of the broth or how much broth base you add, you'll need to eliminate or cut back on the salt. Rice cooking times can vary greatly, depending on the type of rice used and even the brand.

Stovetop Rice

1½ cups long-grain brown rice   **Water**
½ teaspoon salt

1 Place the rice and salt in a saucepan and cover with enough water to come about 1 inch above the rice. Bring to a boil, then reduce heat to low, cover, and cook for 20 minutes.

2 Turn off the heat, and let stand, covered, for 10 minutes.

Oven-Baked Rice

3 cups hot water   **½ teaspoon salt**
1½ cups rice   **1 tablespoon vegan margarine**

1 Preheat the oven to 350°F. Combine ingredients in a 2-quart baking dish.

2 Cover tightly and bake until the rice is tender and the water is absorbed, 45 to 55 minutes.

Note: Here are two more tried-and-true ways to cook rice. One is to make your rice in a rice cooker. If you make lots of rice, this can be a practical investment. Another method that I used when I worked in restaurants is to cook rice the way you make pasta. That is, bring a large pot of salted water to a boil. Add rice and cook at a rolling simmer until the rice is tender. Test for doneness the way you do pasta, by spooning out some and tasting. When the rice is tender, simply drain in a colander the way you drain pasta. These methods work for other grains, as well.

Three-Grain Bread

<50¢
per serving

Bread Machine Version

Makes 1 loaf

This bread machine recipe goes together quickly and makes a delicious golden loaf that we enjoy toasted for breakfast. Using a bread machine cuts down on labor and uses less energy than the oven. Best of all, once you combine all the ingredients, you just press a button and forget about it until it's done baking.

1⅓ cups warm water

1 tablespoon plus 1 teaspoon
    vegan margarine, softened

3 tablespoons sugar

1½ teaspoons salt

2½ cups bread flour

1 cup fine yellow cornmeal

½ cup brown rice flour

2½ teaspoons instant yeast

1 Place the ingredients in the bread pan insert in the following order: water, margarine, sugar, salt, bread flour, cornmeal, and rice flour. Make an indentation and add the yeast.

2 Place the insert in the bread maker and close the lid. Operate according to the manufacturer's instructions to obtain a light-colored 2-pound loaf.

3 When the loaf is done, remove it from pan and set it aside on a rack to cool for 30 minutes before slicing.

Conventional Oven Version

Makes 1 loaf

Here's the same bread recipe adapted for making in a regular oven instead of a bread machine. The cornmeal gives this bread great flavor and a slightly coarse texture that makes it ideal for serving with a stew or hearty soup.

2½ cups bread flour

1 cup fine yellow cornmeal

½ cup brown rice flour

2½ teaspoons instant yeast

1½ teaspoons salt

1⅓ cups warm water

3 tablespoons sugar

1 tablespoon plus 1 teaspoon
    vegan margarine, softened

1 In a large bowl, combine the bread flour, cornmeal, rice flour, yeast, and salt. Mix until well combined.

2 In a separate large bowl, combine the water, sugar, and margarine, stirring to blend. Add about half the flour mixture to the liquid mixture, stirring to combine. Work in the remaining flour mixture until combined, then turn out the dough onto a lightly floured work surface. Knead the dough until it is smooth and elastic, about 8 minutes.

3 Place the dough in a large lightly oiled bowl. Turn the dough to coat it with oil, and cover it with plastic wrap. Let the dough rise in a warm place until doubled, about 1 hour. Lightly oil a 9-inch loaf pan and set it aside. Test your dough by poking it with your finger: If it leaves an indentation from your finger, it's risen enough and is ready for the next step.

4 Punch the dough down and turn it out onto a lightly floured work surface. Shape the dough into a loaf and place it in the prepared pan. Cover with plastic wrap. Set aside in a warm place and let rise again for about 45 minutes.

5 Preheat the oven to 375°F. Bake the bread until golden brown, 45 to 50 minutes. The bread is done if it sounds hollow when tapped on the bottom of the loaf. Cool on a wire rack for 30 minutes before slicing.

Simple Simmered Seitan

<50¢
per serving

Makes about 2 pounds

Unlike the traditional and time-consuming "knead and rinse" method of making seitan, this shortcut recipe uses wheat gluten flour, also known as vital wheat gluten, instead of regular whole wheat flour. Use this seitan in any recipe calling for seitan. After cooling completely, if not using right away, it can be wrapped tightly and frozen for future use.

Seitan
1¾ cups wheat gluten flour (vital
   wheat gluten)
⅓ cup nutritional yeast
1 teaspoon onion powder
1 teaspoon sweet paprika
½ teaspoon salt
1½ cups water or vegetable stock
   (page 45)
¼ cup soy sauce
2 tablespoons olive oil

Simmering Broth
7 cups water
1 medium onion, quartered
2 garlic cloves, crushed
¼ cup soy sauce

❶ **Make the seitan:** In a large bowl, combine the flour, yeast, onion powder, paprika, and salt. In a medium bowl, combine the water, soy sauce, and oil.

❷ Add the wet ingredients to the dry ingredients, stirring to make a soft dough.

❸ Knead for 3 minutes, then let rest for 5 minutes. Divide the dough into 2 to 4 pieces (depending on your needs).

❹ **Make the simmering broth:** In a large saucepan, combine the water, onion, garlic, and soy sauce. Add the seitan pieces to the liquid and bring just to a simmer. Cook for 1 hour. Do not let the liquid come to a boil. The seitan can be allowed to cool in the liquid and then refrigerated until needed for recipes. Seitan keeps well in the refrigerator for 3 to 4 days or in the freezer for 2 to 3 weeks.

Baked Seitan Loaf

< 50¢
per serving

Makes about 2 pounds

This versatile seitan loaf can be chilled and thinly sliced to use in sandwiches and sautés or chopped or diced to use in stews, stir-fries, and chili.

½ cup cooked or canned white
    beans, drained and rinsed
¼ cup soy sauce
1 tablespoon olive oil
1¼ cups vegetable stock (page 45)
2 cups wheat gluten flour (vital
    wheat gluten)

⅓ cup nutritional yeast
2 teaspoons onion powder
1 teaspoon garlic powder
½ teaspoon salt

1 Preheat the oven to 350°F. In a blender or food processor, combine the beans, soy sauce, oil, and stock and blend until smooth.

2 In a large bowl, combine the flour, yeast, onion powder, garlic powder, and salt. Mix to combine. Stir the wet mixture into the dry mixture to make a soft dough. Knead for 3 minutes, then shape into an oval loaf.

3 Place the loaf on an oiled sheet of foil and enclose it in the foil. Place the loaf in a 10-inch baking pan. Add an inch of water to the baking pan and tightly cover the entire pan with foil. Bake until firm, about 1 hour and 45 minutes.

Cutlets on the Cheap

Makes 8 cutlets

Make a batch of these cutlets and then cool and refrigerate some to use right away. Individually wrap and freeze the rest for future use. Infinitely versatile, these cutlets can be sautéed and sauced in a variety of ways. See the sidebar on the opposite page for some ideas.

Cooking Broth

8 cups water

¼ cup soy sauce

1 medium yellow onion, quartered

3 garlic cloves, crushed

2 tablespoons vegetable broth base (see Note)

Cutlets

½ cup cooked or canned white beans, drained and rinsed

1 cup cold vegetable stock (page 45)

2 tablespoons soy sauce

1⅓ cups wheat gluten flour (vital wheat gluten)

⅓ cup nutritional yeast

1 teaspoon garlic powder

½ teaspoon onion powder

❶ **Make the broth:** In a large pot, combine the water, soy sauce, onion, garlic, and broth base, and set aside.

❷ **Make the cutlets:** Puree the beans in a food processor until smooth. Add the stock and soy sauce and process until blended. Add the flour, yeast, garlic powder, and onion powder, and process until well blended.

❸ Turn the dough out onto a lightly floured work surface and knead for 5 minutes. Cover and set aside to rest for 5 minutes. Stretch the dough into a rectangle about ½-inch thick. Cut the dough into 8 pieces. Flatten each piece into a thin cutlet. You can do this with your hands or by placing each cutlet between two sheets of plastic wrap and rolling flat with a rolling pin.

❹ Add the cutlets to the pot with the broth mixture and bring just to a simmer over medium-low heat. Cover and simmer for 1 hour, turning about halfway through. Do not allow the broth to boil. Remove from the heat and allow the cutlets to cool in the broth. You can refrigerate the cutlets in the broth or remove them from the broth and wrap them well, then refrigerate or freeze until needed. Properly stored, they will keep well for about 3 days in the refrigerator or several weeks in the freezer. The cutlets can then be sautéed in a small amount of oil until golden brown and topped with a sauce or cut into strips or chunks to use in recipes. The cooking broth can also be frozen and reused for future batches of cutlets

Note: Vegetable broth base is available in both paste and powder form under various brand names and can be found in well-stocked supermarkets and natural food stores.

Ten Ways to Serve Cutlets on the Cheap

One of the best things about Cutlets on the Cheap is that once you've made a batch (or two) the sky's the limit on how to serve them. To get you started, here are ten ways to enjoy these tasty (and cheap) cutlets.

1. Top the cutlets with Creamy Mushroom Gravy (page 31).

2. Saute the cutlets with red wine and sliced mushrooms, then stir in some creamy mushroom gravy for a rich wine sauce.

3. Saute the cutlets with white wine, garlic, lemon juice, and capers for a luscious picatta.

4. Top with marinara sauce and a sprinkling of vegan cheese, then run under the broiler to melt the cheese.

5. Slice the cutlets into strips and add them to the Quick Lo Mein (page 123).

6. Cut into strips and add to the Asian Noodle Soup (page 70).

7. Cut into strips and use in the Build-Your-Own Fajitas (page 188).

8. Use cutlets instead of seitan for the Cajun-Spiced Seitan Po' Boys (page 181).

9. Use cutlets instead of the sausage patties in the Savory Sausage and Peppers (page 141).

10. Use cutlets instead of Poloenta in the Polenta with Pan-Seared Mushrooms and Tomato Sauce (page 138).

Close to Mom's Sausage Patties

< 50¢ per serving

Makes 6 patties

Even during the days when I still ate meat, I could never quite dupli-
cate my mom's homemade Italian sausage. Now vegan for over twenty
years, I'm still working on matching her spicy fennel-rich seasonings in
my vegan sausage. Though I consider it a work-in-progress, this version
is as close as I've come. I think Mom would be proud. Both the patties
and the links variation make great sandwiches, especially when topped
with sauteed onions and bell peppers and a bit of mustard or ketchup.
They're also good as a main dish or chopped and added to marinara
sauce for pasta.

1 cup wheat gluten flour (vital
   wheat gluten)

3 tablespoons tapioca flour (see
   Note)

2 teaspoons sweet paprika

1½ teaspoons whole fennel seeds

1 teaspoon ground fennel seed

1 teaspoon onion powder

1 teaspoon garlic powder

1 teaspoon crushed red pepper

½ teaspoon ground cayenne

½ teaspoon salt

¼ teaspoon black pepper

⅔ cup cooked or canned dark red
   kidney beans, drained and
   rinsed

¾ cup water

2 tablespoons soy sauce

3 tablespoons olive oil

1 Preheat the oven to 350°F.

2 In a food processor, combine the wheat gluten flour, tapioca flour, paprika,
whole and ground fennel seed, onion powder, garlic powder, crushed red
pepper, cayenne, salt, and black pepper. Pulse to mix.

3 In a medium bowl, coarsely mash the beans, then add them to the food
processor. Pour in the water, soy sauce, and 2 tablespoons of the oil and
process until well mixed.

4 Shape the mixture into 6 patties about ¼ inch thick and wrap each in foil.
Arrange them in a single layer in a 9 x 13-inch baking pan and add about
¼ inch of water to the pan. Cover tightly with foil. Bake for 45 minutes,
turning once about halfway through. Remove the patties from the pan,
unwrap them, and set them on a platter.

5 Heat the remaining 1 tablespoon of oil in a large skillet over medium heat. Add the patties and cook until browned on both sides, about 4 minutes per side. If not using right away, cool the patties to room temperature, then wrap tightly and refrigerate until needed. They will keep in the refrigerator for up to 3 days or frozen for several weeks.

Variation

Sausage Links: To make links instead of patties, shape the mixture into thin logs and wrap each log in foil. Arrange the foil-wrapped logs in the baking pan and add about ¼ inch of water to the pan. Cover tightly with foil and bake for 45 minutes, then proceed with the recipe.

Note: Tapioca flour adds firmness and improves the texture of the sausage and pepperoni. It is available in natural food stores and can often be found in bulk.

Big Stick Pepperoni

< 50¢ per serving

Makes about 1 pound

This is a vegan version of the "big stick" pepperoni my mother used to buy when I was a kid. Use this tasty and versatile faux pepperoni in soups, sandwiches, salads, pilafs, pasta dishes, and of course, as a pizza topping. Flavorful, protein rich, and easy to make, it costs a small fraction of commercial vegan pepperoni products. Liquid smoke is a seasoning liquid, available in supermarkets, that adds a smoky flavor to foods.

1 cup wheat gluten flour (vital wheat gluten)
1/4 cup nutritional yeast
3 tablespoons tapioca flour (see Note, page 55)
2 teaspoons smoked paprika
1 teaspoon ground fennel seed
3/4 teaspoon garlic powder
3/4 teaspoon onion powder
1/2 teaspoon whole fennel seeds

1/2 teaspoon crushed red pepper
1/2 teaspoon ground cayenne
1/2 teaspoon salt
1/4 teaspoon black pepper
3/4 cup water
2 tablespoons ketchup
2 tablespoons olive oil
1 tablespoon soy sauce
1 teaspoon liquid smoke

1. Preheat the oven to 350°F. In a medium bowl, combine the wheat gluten flour, yeast, tapioca flour, and spices. Set aside.

2. In a small bowl, combine the water, ketchup, oil, soy sauce, and liquid smoke, stirring to blend. Add the wet ingredients to the dry ingredients and mix well.

3. Knead for a few minutes, then divide in half and roll into 2 logs about 7 inches long. Wrap the logs in foil, twisting the ends to seal.

4. Place the logs in a 9-inch baking pan, add about 1/2 inch of water to the pan, and cover tightly with foil. Bake for 1 hour, turning halfway through. Unwrap and cool for about 15 minutes, then refrigerate to firm up, about 1 to 2 hours. Use a serrated knife to cut into thin slices. Use as is or pan-fry as needed. If not using right away, wrap tightly and store in the refrigerator, where they will keep for 3 to 4 days, or freeze for 3 to 4 weeks.

Wheatballs

< 50¢ per serving

Makes about 28 wheatballs

Chickpeas and mushrooms combine with wheat gluten flour, bread crumbs, and seasonings to create mini-meatballs with great taste and texture. Serve them with Spaghetti Marinara (page 110) or add them to Minestrone Soup (page 66). They also make a great sandwich and they freeze well, too.

1½ cups cooked or 1 (15.5-ounce) can chickpeas, drained and rinsed

1 cup chopped white mushrooms

2 garlic cloves, minced

2 tablespoons minced fresh parsley

2 tablespoons tomato paste

2 tablespoons soy sauce

1 tablespoon water

1½ tablespoons olive oil, plus more for cooking

½ cup dry bread crumbs

½ cup wheat gluten flour (vital wheat gluten)

¼ cup nutritional yeast

1 teaspoon dried basil

¾ teaspoon dried oregano

½ teaspoon paprika

½ teaspoon salt

¼ teaspoon black pepper

1 In a food processor, combine the chickpeas, mushrooms, garlic, and parsley and pulse until coarsely ground, but not pureed. Add the remaining ingredients and pulse to combine.

2 Use a rubber spatula to scrape the mixture into a large bowl and knead the mixture until well blended, about 2 minutes.

3 Pinch off a small piece of the mixture, press it together in your hand, then roll into a 1½-inch ball. Repeat with the remaining mixture.

4 In a large skillet, heat a thin layer of oil over medium heat. Add the wheatballs, in batches if necessary, and cook until browned all over, moving them in the pan as needed for even browning, about 5 minutes.

5 Repeat until all the wheatballs are cooked. They are now ready to use in recipes. If not using right away, cool completely, then cover and refrigerate or freeze until needed. Properly stored, they will keep in the refrigerator for 3 to 4 days or in the freezer for 3 to 4 weeks.

Variation

Baked Wheatballs: Instead of browning the wheatballs in a skillet, you can bake them in an oiled baking pan at 375°F for 25 minutes, turning once halfway through.

Smoky Tempeh Bits

<50¢ per serving

Makes about 2 cups

These versatile tempeh bits can be used on top of salads à la "bacon bits," added to rice or noodle dishes, or included as a tasty filling ingredient for wrap sandwiches or burritos. They also add great flavor and texture to some of the recipes in this book such as Caldo Verde (page 67) and White Bean and Barley "Risotto" with Kale and Tempeh (page 135). If you prefer a more straightforward flavor, omit the liquid smoke. If you want to make the tempeh spicy, add some hot sauce or chile paste to the seasoning mixture.

8 ounces tempeh

3 tablespoons soy sauce

3 tablespoons water

1½ teaspoons liquid smoke

1 tablespoon olive oil

❶ In a medium saucepan of simmering water, cook the tempeh over medium heat for 20 minutes. Drain and pat dry. Crumble or chop the tempeh into small bits and set aside. In a small bowl, combine the soy sauce, water, and liquid smoke. Set aside.

❷ In a medium skillet, heat the oil over medium-high heat. Add the tempeh and cook, stirring until nicely browned, about 5 minutes. Add the soy sauce mixture, stirring to coat the tempeh. Continue cooking until the liquid is absorbed and the tempeh is evenly coated. Remove from the heat. The tempeh is now ready to use in recipes. If not using right away, cool completely, then cover and refrigerate or freeze until needed. Properly stored, it will keep in the refrigerator for 3 to 4 days or in the freezer for 3 to 4 weeks.

Double Pie Crust

<50¢
per serving

Makes 2 pie crusts

This recipe makes enough dough for a double crust, which I encourage you to make even when you only need a single crust. If you don't need to use two crusts, simply shape the remaining dough into a disk, wrap it well, and freeze until needed, then thaw in the refrigerator. It's like money in the bank—well, almost. (Note: For a savory pie crust, omit the sugar.)

3 cups all-purpose flour	⅔ cup cold vegan margarine, cut
1½ teaspoons sugar	into ¼-inch dice
1 teaspoon salt	½ cup cold water

1 In a food processor, combine the flour, sugar, and salt and pulse to blend.

2 Add the margarine and pulse to cut the margarine into the flour mixture until it resembles coarse crumbs.

3 Add the water and process just until the dough holds together, adding a splash more water if needed.

4 Turn the dough out onto a lightly floured work surface and use your hands to shape it into a ball, then divide the dough in half. Shape each half into a ball and flatten each into a 1-inch-thick disk. Wrap each disk tightly in plastic wrap and refrigerate for at least 30 minutes or until needed. Properly stored, it will keep in the refrigerator for up to a week or frozen for up to 2 months.

Soup and Stew Savvy

here some soups are regarded as "light" fare, and are often served for lunch or as a first course, there are also hearty soups that are known for being nutritious as well as budget stretching. This chapter is filled with the tempting soups such as Minestrone Soup with Tiny "Meatballs" (page 66), Asian Noodle Soup (page 70), and Southwestern Black Bean and Corn Chowder (page 68) that combine beans, grains, and vegetables to make soups that are substantial enough to enjoy as one-dish meals.

In addition to hearty soups, this chapter contains recipes for satisfying stews and chilis, including Cincinnati Suburb Chili (page 80), a vegan variation of five-way Cincinnati chili, and Southern New Year's Stew (page 76), inspired by the tradition of eating black-eyed peas and collards for good fortune in the coming year.

All of the soup and stew recipes in this chapter were carefully chosen for their hearty "one-dish" meal appeal. And, like most soups and stews, they taste even better the next day, making leftovers a pleasure.

Taking Stock

Prepared commercial vegetable broths and stocks can be expensive, so for the most economical choice, use a homemade stock such as the one on page 45, or use water with some vegetable base added. There are several good-quality vegetable bases available in both powder and paste form. If you're a fan of the more expensive prepared broths sold in cans or aseptic containers, consider diluting them by half with water (freezing what you don't use) to get twice as much for your money.

Red Bean Gazpacho Anytime

<$1.00 per serving

Makes 4 to 6 servings

Gazpacho is typically summertime fare when fresh tomatoes and other vegetables are ripe for the picking. Now you can satisfy your gazpacho craving even when fresh tomatoes are at a premium with this quick and easy recipe. Choose a mild, medium, or hot salsa, according to your own preference. Instead of using tomato juice you can substitute a vegetable juice blend for added flavor dimension and nutrients.

1 cucumber, peeled, halved, and seeded
½ cup finely chopped red onion
1 (16-ounce) jar chunky tomato salsa
1½ cups cooked or 1 (15.5-ounce) can dark red kidney beans, drained and rinsed

1 tablespoon red wine vinegar (optional)
1 quart tomato or blended vegetable juice
Salt and black pepper

1 Finely chop the cucumber and place it in a large bowl. Add the onion, then stir in the salsa, beans, vinegar, if using, and tomato juice, and season with salt and pepper to taste.

2 Refrigerate for 2 hours to chill and allow flavors to blend. Serve chilled.

Splurge a Little
Garnish with diced avocado.

Almost-Instant Chickpea-Tomato Soup

<$1.00 per serving

Makes 4 servings

This creamy, rich-tasting soup couldn't be easier or more economical. It's also good served chilled.

1½ cups cooked or 1 (15.5-ounce) can chickpeas, drained and rinsed

2 garlic cloves, crushed

1 (14.5-ounce) can crushed or diced tomatoes

1 teaspoon ground cumin

2 tablespoons fresh lemon juice

2 tablespoons olive oil

1 cup plain unsweetened soy milk

Salt

Ground cayenne

2 tablespoons minced fresh cilantro or parsley

❶ In a high-speed blender, combine the chickpeas and garlic and process until finely ground.

❷ Add the tomatoes, cumin, lemon juice, oil, ½ cup of the soy milk, and salt and cayenne to taste. Blend until smooth.

❸ Add as much of the remaining ½ cup of soy milk as needed to achieve desired consistency—not too thin or too thick—and blend until smooth and creamy. Taste and adjust the seasonings, adding more salt and cayenne, if necessary.

❹ Transfer the soup to a large saucepan over medium heat and cook, stirring, until hot, about 5 minutes. If serving hot, ladle into bowls, top with minced cilantro, and serve at once. If serving chilled, let the soup cool to room temperature, then transfer to a serving bowl. Cover and refrigerate until chilled, about 3 hours. Then ladle into soup bowls and garnish with the cilantro.

Splurge a Little

Garnish with chopped pitted kalamata olives.

Pasta e Fagioli

<$1.00 per serving>

Makes 4 servings

Literally "pasta and beans," pasta e fagioli (also called pasta "fazool") is a stick-to-your-ribs comfort food Italian dish that tastes even better the day after it is made. My mother served this for dinner every Friday and it was so delicious it never occurred to me she made it to be thrifty. Mom usually used Roman beans, also called borlotti or cranberry beans, which look like large pinto beans. She sometimes added a small amount of pepperoni for extra flavor when it was on hand. For a heartier version, add an extra cup of cooked beans or garnish each bowl with 2 tablespoons of diced Big Stick Pepperoni (page 56).

2 tablespoons olive oil
3 garlic cloves, minced
1 (28-ounce) can crushed tomatoes
1½ cups cooked or 1 (15.5-ounce) can cannellini beans, drained and rinsed
½ teaspoon dried oregano
½ teaspoon dried basil
1 bay leaf
2 cups vegetable stock (page 45)
Salt and black pepper
8 ounces elbow macaroni or other small pasta
1 tablespoon minced fresh parsley

1. In a large pot, heat the oil over medium heat. Add the garlic and cook until softened, about 1 minute. Reduce the heat to low and stir in the tomatoes. Add the beans, oregano, basil, bay leaf, stock, and salt and pepper to taste. (The amount of salt needed depends on the saltiness of your stock.) Simmer over low heat for about 20 minutes.

2. In a large pot of boiling salted water, cook the macaroni over medium-high heat, stirring occasionally, until it is al dente, about 7 minutes. Drain well and add to the bean mixture along with the parsley.

3. Simmer gently to blend flavors and finish cooking the pasta, about 10 minutes. Remove the bay leaf and discard. Taste and adjust the seasonings, if necessary, before serving. Serve hot.

Mom's Bread and Cabbage Soup

<$1.00 per serving

Makes 4 to 6 servings

Thanks to my mother's thrift, many naturally vegan soups, pastas, and other dishes made regular appearances at my house when I was growing up. This classic Italian *piatto povero* ("peasant dish") remains one of my favorites. Sliced Italian bread placed in the bottom of the bowls is the key to this soup, adding heartiness and texture. (My mother always used the ends of old, nearly stale bread loaves for this recipe.)

4 to 6 slices Italian bread

1 tablespoon olive oil

1 large yellow onion, chopped

2 garlic cloves, minced

1 small head cabbage, chopped

1 teaspoon dried savory

1 teaspoon dried basil

1 (14.5-ounce) can diced tomatoes, undrained

1½ cups cooked or 1 (15.5-ounce) can Great Northern or other white beans, drained and rinsed

4½ cups vegetable stock (page 45)

Salt and black pepper

1 Set the bread slices on the kitchen counter to dry out while you make the soup.

2 In a large pot, heat the oil over medium heat. Add the onion, cover, and cook, until the onion is softened, about 5 minutes. Add the garlic and cabbage and cook, stirring, for 5 minutes.

3 Add the savory, basil, tomatoes with their juice, beans, stock, and salt and pepper to taste. (The amount of salt needed depends on the saltiness of your stock.) Bring to a boil, then reduce heat to low and simmer, uncovered, until the vegetables are tender, about 45 minutes.

4 When ready to serve, place a slice of bread in the bottom of each bowl and ladle the soup on top. Serve hot.

Minestrone Soup with Tiny "Meatballs"

<$1.50 per serving

Makes 6 servings

One of the best things about a minestrone soup is that you can vary it according to your personal taste and what's on hand. The "meatballs" in this version add great flavor and texture, but you can leave them out if you prefer. In addition to changing up some of the vegetables, you can add cooked pasta or rice when ready to serve, and even a swirl of pesto for added flavor.

1 tablespoon olive oil
1 medium yellow onion, chopped
2 medium carrots, chopped
1 celery rib, chopped
2 garlic cloves, minced
1 (14.5-ounce) can diced tomatoes, undrained
½ teaspoon dried basil
½ teaspoon dried oregano
5 cups vegetable stock (page 45)
Salt and black pepper

2 medium zucchini, cut into ½-inch dice
1½ cups cooked or 1 (15.5-ounce) can cannellini beans or other white beans, drained and rinsed
3 cups chopped fresh spinach
2 tablespoons minced fresh parsley
12 to 16 small cooked Wheatballs (page 57)

❶ In a large pot, heat the oil over medium heat. Add the onion, carrots, celery, and garlic, cover, and cook until softened, about 10 minutes.

❷ Add the tomatoes with their juice, basil, oregano, stock, and salt and pepper to taste. (The amount of salt needed depends on the saltiness of your stock.) Bring to a boil, then reduce the heat to medium-low and simmer for 20 minutes.

❸ Add the zucchini and beans and cook until the zucchini is softened, another 15 minutes.

❹ Stir in the spinach and simmer until wilted, about 2 minutes. Just before serving, add the parsley and the wheatballs and taste and adjust seasonings, if necessary. Serve hot.

Caldo Verde

Makes 4 to 6 servings

White beans and potatoes play supporting roles, but kale is the star of this satisfying and economical Portuguese soup. The addition of Smoky Tempeh Bits (page 58) add great texture and flavor to the soup. For a variation, instead of the tempeh, you can instead add some sautéed sliced Big Stick Pepperoni (page 56) to the soup when ready to serve.

2 tablespoons olive oil

1 large Spanish onion, chopped

3 garlic cloves, minced

1½ pounds russet potatoes, cut into ½-inch dice

8 cups vegetable stock (page 45) or water

1 teaspoon dried marjoram

½ teaspoon crushed red pepper

1 teaspoon salt, or to taste

1½ cups cooked or 1 (15.5-ounce) can white beans, drained and rinsed

6 cups finely chopped kale

¼ cup dry white wine or sherry (optional)

Black pepper

½ cup Smoky Tempeh Bits (page 58)

1 In a large pot, heat 1 tablespoon of the oil over medium heat. Add the onion, cover, and cook until softened, about 5 minutes. Add the garlic and cook 1 minute longer. Add the potatoes, stock, marjoram, crushed red pepper, and about 1 teaspoon of salt, and bring to a boil. Reduce heat to medium and simmer for 20 minutes.

2 Stir in the beans. Taste and adjust the seasonings, if necessary. (You may need to add more salt if you used water instead of stock.) Keep the soup at a low simmer.

3 In a large skillet, heat the remaining 1 tablespoon oil. Add the kale and the wine, if using. Season with black pepper to taste. Add ¼ cup of the stock from the soup. Cook, stirring until the kale is wilted, about 5 minutes. Stir the kale mixture into the soup and simmer for 10 to 12 minutes or until the vegetables are tender and the flavors are well blended.

4 When ready to serve, stir the tempeh bits into the soup. Serve hot.

Southwestern Black Bean and Corn Chowder

Makes 4 to 6 servings

The flavors of the Southwest converge in this satisfying chowder. Serve with a bowl of extra tortilla chips on the side.

1 tablespoon olive oil

1 medium yellow onion, chopped

2 garlic cloves, minced

3 cups cooked or 2 (15.5-ounce) cans black beans, drained and rinsed

1 (14-ounce) can diced fire-roasted tomatoes, undrained

1 (4-ounce) can chopped mild green chiles, drained

1½ cups fresh or thawed frozen corn kernels

1 teaspoon chili powder

½ teaspoon ground cumin

½ teaspoon smoked paprika (optional)

3 cups vegetable stock (page 45)

Salt and black pepper

Tortilla chips

1 In a large pot, heat the oil over medium heat. Add the onion and garlic, cover, and cook until softened, about 5 minutes.

2 Stir in the beans, tomatoes with their juice, chiles, corn, chili powder, cumin, and paprika, if using. Add the stock and season with salt and pepper to taste. (The amount of salt needed depends on the saltiness of your stock.) Simmer until the chowder is hot and the flavors have developed, 30 to 40 minutes.

3 To serve, ladle the chowder into bowls and top each bowl with tortilla chips.

Splurge a Little

After ladling the chowder into bowls, garnish each with a few tablespoons of diced ripe avocado squeezed with a little lime juice.

Summer Garden Soup

Makes 6 servings

You can adapt this satisfying soup according to what's on hand or in season. Good additions include chard or spinach, added near the end of cooking time. If fresh ripe tomatoes are not in season, substitute a can of diced tomatoes instead. For a more substantial soup, add some cooked rice or pasta when ready to serve. Note: If you won't be eating all of the soup at one meal, rather than adding cooked rice or pasta to the pot of soup, it's best to add it to the individual bowls and then pour the hot soup on top; otherwise any leftover rice or pasta in the soup will absorb the broth and expand.

2 tablespoons olive oil

1 medium onion, chopped

1 medium carrot, chopped

2 garlic cloves, minced

3 small white potatoes

2 cups green beans, trimmed and cut into 1-inch pieces

1 medium zucchini, chopped

1 medium yellow squash, chopped

3 ripe plum tomatoes, seeded and chopped

5 cups vegetable stock (page 45)

Salt and black pepper

1½ cups cooked or 1 (15.5-ounce) can white beans, drained and rinsed

¼ cup chopped fresh basil

¼ cup chopped fresh parsley

1 In a large pot, heat the oil over medium heat. Add the onion, carrot, garlic, potatoes, and green beans. Cover and cook for 7 minutes, stirring occasionally.

2 Add the zucchini, yellow squash, tomatoes, and stock. Season with salt and pepper to taste. (The amount of salt needed depends on the saltiness of your stock.) Cover and simmer until the vegetables are tender, about 30 minutes.

3 Stir in the beans, basil, and parsley. Taste and adjust seasonings, if necessary. Serve hot.

Asian Noodle Soup

<$1.50 per serving

Makes 4 to 6 servings

Inspired by the traditional Vietnamese noodle soup called *pho*, this meatless version is made with seitan. The recipe calls for linguine since most everyone has it on hand, but you can use rice noodles if you prefer. For those who like to add extra heat, include a bottle of sriracha, a widely available Asian hot chile sauce, at the table.

8 ounces linguine

1 tablespoon neutral vegetable oil

8 ounces seitan (page 50), cut into cut into ¼-inch strips

1 small yellow onion, cut into ¼-inch slices

2 garlic cloves, minced

2 teaspoons grated fresh ginger

2 tablespoons hoisin sauce

2 tablespoons soy sauce

5 cups vegetable stock (page 45) or water

2 tablespoons rice vinegar

½ teaspoon sriracha chili sauce (see headnote), or to taste

1 cup fresh bean sprouts

3 green onions, minced

½ cup coarsely chopped fresh cilantro

❶ In a large pot of boiling salted water, cook the linguine over medium-high heat, stirring occasionally, until al dente, about 8 minutes. Drain, rinse under cold water, and set aside.

❷ In a large skillet, heat the oil over medium-high heat, add the seitan strips, and cook until browned all over. Remove the seitan from the skillet and set aside.

❸ Reheat the same skillet over medium heat. Add the onion, cover, and cook until softened, about 5 minutes. Stir in the garlic and ginger and cook for 30 seconds.

❹ Scrape the onion mixture into a large pot. Stir in the hoisin sauce and soy sauce. Add the stock and bring to a boil. Reduce heat to low and simmer for 15 minutes.

❺ Stir in the cooked seitan, noodles, vinegar, and sriracha, and simmer for 5 minutes to heat through and develop the flavors.

❻ Divide the soup among individual bowls and top each bowl with some bean sprouts, green onions, and cilantro. Serve at once with extra sriracha on the side.

Splurge a Little

Use rice noodles instead of linguine. Add dark miso paste to enrich the broth. Use fresh lime juice instead of rice vinegar.

Recycle Those Vegetables

If you make vegetable stock using fresh vegetables only (as opposed to using peelings, stems, and so on) you may be hesitant to toss those cooked veggies out once you strain them from the stock. Here's an idea: Puree the cooked vegetables in a blender or food processor. You can then stir them right back into the stock for a thick, rich stock, or portion and freeze the vegetable puree to enrich soups, stews, and casseroles.

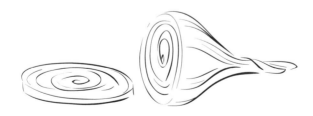

Peanutty Pumpkin Stew

<$1.50 per serving

Makes 4 to 6 servings

You can stretch this delicious and versatile stew further by serving it over cooked rice or quinoa. A small amount of curry and chiles add distinct flavor notes without being overpowering; however, for a more child-friendly version, you can leave them out.

1 tablespoon olive oil

1 medium onion, chopped

1 medium carrot, chopped

1 medium potato, chopped

1 garlic clove, minced

1 (14.5-ounce) can crushed tomatoes

1 (16-ounce) can solid-pack pumpkin

⅓ cup creamy peanut butter

2 tablespoons soy sauce

2 teaspoons hot or mild curry powder

2 cups vegetable stock (page 45)

1½ cups cooked or 1 (15.5-ounce) can kidney beans, drained and rinsed

1 (4-ounce) can chopped hot or mild green chiles, drained

1 cup thawed frozen peas

¼ cup chopped unsalted roasted peanuts

2 tablespoons minced fresh parsley

❶ In a large pot, heat the oil over medium heat. Add the onion, carrot, potato, and garlic. Cover and cook until softened, about 7 minutes.

❷ Stir in the tomatoes, pumpkin, peanut butter, soy sauce, curry powder, and stock, stirring after each addition until well blended. Add the beans and chiles and simmer, stirring occasionally, until the stew is hot and the flavors are blended, about 20 minutes.

❸ Shortly before serving, stir in the peas. Serve hot, garnished with peanuts and parsley.

Vegetable Lentil Stew

<$1.00
per serving

Makes 6 to 8 servings

Usually when I make lentil soup, I include the basic vegetable mirepoix of onion, carrot, and celery, but it occurred to me that if I added a few extra veggies, what was once a lentil-dominant hearty soup could be transformed into a luscious stew with a wonderful balance of vegetables and lentils, making it a terrific and thrifty main dish. I use brown lentils in this stew because they are cheaper than the other varieties and are readily available in supermarkets.

2 tablespoons olive oil

1 large yellow onion, chopped

3 garlic cloves, minced

1 teaspoon dried savory

½ teaspoon ground fennel seed

½ teaspoon dried thyme

½ teaspoon smoked paprika

8 ounces brown lentils, picked over, rinsed, and drained

6 cups vegetable stock (page 45)

¼ to ½ cup dry red wine (optional)

1 (28-ounce) can crushed tomatoes

2 medium Yukon Gold potatoes, chopped

2 medium carrots, chopped

1 medium parsnip, peeled and chopped

1 celery rib, chopped

1 teaspoon salt

¼ teaspoon black pepper

3 cups finely chopped cabbage

❶ In a large pot, heat the oil over medium heat. Add the onion and garlic. Cover and cook until the onion is soft, 5 minutes. Stir in the savory, fennel, thyme, paprika, lentils, and stock and bring to a boil. Reduce heat to medium and simmer for 10 minutes.

❷ Stir in the wine, if using, tomatoes, potatoes, carrots, parsnip, and celery. Add salt and pepper. Increase the heat to bring back to a simmer, then reduce heat to medium, cover, and simmer for 20 minutes.

❸ Add the cabbage. Taste and adjust seasonings, if necessary. Simmer for about 20 minutes longer or until the vegetables and lentils are tender. Serve hot.

Call It Cassoulet

<$1.50 per serving

Makes 4 to 6 servings

Sometimes a name makes all the difference. When I make this penny-pinching dish and tell my husband we're having bean stew, he says "Oh." But when I call it cassoulet, he says, "Ahhh!" Take my advice: Call it cassoulet.

1 tablespoon olive oil

2 medium carrots, cut into ¼-inch slices

1 celery rib, chopped

1 medium yellow onion, chopped

2 garlic cloves, crushed

1 (28-ounce) can diced tomatoes, undrained

4 cups cooked or 3 (15.5-ounce) cans white beans, drained and rinsed

2 cups vegetable stock (page 45)

1 teaspoon dried savory

½ teaspoon dried thyme

½ teaspoon dried marjoram

Salt and black pepper

1 cup chopped or sliced Big Stick Pepperoni (page 56; optional)

Toasted croutons (recipe follows)

1 In a large pot, heat the oil over medium heat. Add the carrots, celery, onion, and garlic. Cover and cook until softened, 7 minutes.

2 Stir in the tomatoes, beans, stock, savory, thyme, marjoram, and salt and pepper to taste. (The amount of salt needed depends on the saltiness of your stock.) Bring to a boil, then reduce heat to low and simmer, partially covered, until the vegetables are tender and the flavors have developed, adding more stock or water if needed, about 30 minutes.

3 If desired, just before serving sauté the pepperoni in a medium skillet in a small amount of oil until browned. Add some of the sautéed pepperoni to each serving. Serve hot, garnished with croutons.

Toasted Croutons

In addition to their use in the recipe at left, these croutons make a great addition to salads and soups.

4 (½-inch-thick) slices Italian bread
2 tablespoons olive oil
Salt and black pepper

1 Cut the bread into ½-inch cubes and set aside.

2 In a large skillet, heat the oil over medium heat. Add the bread cubes and cook until lightly browned all over, stirring as needed, about 10 minutes total. Season with salt and pepper to taste. The croutons are now ready to use and are best if eaten on the same day they are made.

Southern
New Year's Stew

<$1.00 per serving

Makes 6 servings

Inspired by the New Year's institution called Hoppin' John, this hearty stew combines black-eyed peas, rice, and collards for a stick-to-your-ribs stew that makes a great one-dish meal. If fresh collards are unavailable substitute another dark green such as kale, or use frozen collards. You can also make this stew using leftover cooked rice—just add it a few minutes before serving time to heat through.

8 ounces collard greens or other dark leafy greens, tough stems removed and coarsely chopped (about 4 cups)
2 tablespoons olive oil
1 large yellow onion, finely chopped
1 celery rib, chopped
1 medium carrot, chopped
3 garlic cloves, minced
4 cups vegetable stock (page 45)

½ cup long-grain brown rice
1 teaspoon dried thyme
¼ teaspoon black pepper
Salt
1 russet potato, chopped
1½ cups cooked or 1 (15.5-ounce) can black-eyed peas, drained and rinsed
Tabasco sauce, for serving

❶ In a large pot of boiling salted water, cook the collards over medium-high heat until tender, about 20 minutes. Drain well and set aside.

❷ In a large pot, heat the oil over medium heat. Add the onion, celery, and carrot, and garlic. Cover and cook, stirring occasionally, until slightly softened, about 5 minutes.

❸ Stir in the stock, rice, thyme, pepper, and salt to taste and bring to a boil. (The amount of salt needed depends on the saltiness of your stock.) Reduce the heat to low and simmer for 15 minutes.

❹ Stir in the potato and black-eyed peas and continue to cook until the vegetables and rice are tender, about 30 minutes. Stir in the cooked collards and taste and adjust seasonings, if necessary. Simmer to heat through and allow the flavors to mingle, about 10 minutes. Serve hot with a bottle of Tabasco at the table.

Sweet Potato Succotash Stew

<$1.50 per serving

Makes 6 servings

This hearty and flavorful stew combines frozen lima beans and corn kernels with sweet potatoes for a colorful and economical meal. Like most stews, this tastes better the day after it is made, so plan to make it ahead and reheat it when ready to serve.

1 tablespoon olive oil

1 large yellow onion, chopped

2 celery ribs, minced

2 large sweet potatoes, peeled and cut into ½-inch dice

3 garlic cloves, minced

1 (14.5-ounce) can diced tomatoes, undrained

2 cups thawed frozen lima beans

3 tablespoons soy sauce

1½ teaspoons spicy brown mustard

1 teaspoon light brown sugar

½ teaspoon ground cumin

½ teaspoon ground allspice

1 teaspoon Tabasco sauce

2 cups vegetable stock (page 45)

¼ teaspoon black pepper

Salt

2 cups thawed frozen corn kernels

½ teaspoon liquid smoke (optional)

1 In a large pot, heat the oil over medium heat. Add the onion and celery. Cover and cook until softened, about 10 minutes. Add the sweet potatoes and garlic. Cover and cook, stirring occasionally, until softened, about 5 minutes.

2 Remove the lid and stir in the tomatoes, lima beans, soy sauce, mustard, sugar, cumin, allspice, and Tabasco. Add the stock, pepper, and salt to taste. (The amount of salt needed depends on the saltiness of your stock.) Bring to a boil, then reduce the heat to low and simmer, uncovered, until the vegetables are tender, stirring occasionally, about 30 minutes.

3 Stir in the corn and simmer for 15 minutes longer. Add the liquid smoke, if using. Taste and adjust seasonings, if necessary. Serve hot.

Black and White Bean Chili

<$1.00 per serving

Makes 4 to 6 servings

This hearty chili made with contrasting beans is enriched by the smoky-spicy flavors of chipotle chile and smoked paprika.

1 tablespoon olive oil

1 large onion, chopped

2 garlic cloves, minced

1 small green bell pepper, finely chopped

1 (28-ounce) can diced tomatoes, undrained

3 cups cooked or 2 (15.5-ounce) cans black beans, drained and rinsed

1½ cups cooked or 1 (15.5-ounce) can cannellini or other white beans, drained and rinsed

1 or 2 chipotle chiles in adobo, minced

2 tablespoons chili powder

1 teaspoon smoked paprika

1 teaspoon ground cumin

½ teaspoon dried oregano

¼ teaspoon black pepper

Salt

1 cup water or tomato juice

1 In a large pot, heat the oil over medium heat. Add the onion, cover, and cook until softened, about 7 minutes. Add the garlic and bell pepper and cook for 1 minute longer.

2 Add all the remaining ingredients and cook, stirring occasionally, until the chili is hot and the flavors have blended, about 45 minutes. Taste and adjust seasonings, if necessary. Serve hot.

French Lentil Chili

<$1.00 per serving

Makes 4 servings

The tiny green lentils known as French lentils have a great texture for chili because they hold their shape instead of getting mushy. Serve with a warm baguette if you want to accentuate the French accent.

1 tablespoon olive oil	1 teaspoon salt
1 medium onion, minced	1 teaspoon ground cumin
1 medium carrot, minced	1 teaspoon dried thyme
1 celery rib, minced	½ teaspoon sugar
3 garlic cloves	¼ teaspoon black pepper
1½ cups French lentils	3 cups water
1 (28-ounce) can crushed tomatoes	1 tablespoon sherry vinegar
2 tablespoons chili powder	(optional)

1 In a large pot, heat the oil over medium heat. Add the onion, carrot, celery, and garlic. Cover and cook until softened, about 7 minutes.

2 Add the lentils, tomatoes, chili powder, salt, cumin, thyme, sugar, pepper, and water. Bring to a boil, then reduce heat to low.

3 Cover and simmer until lentils and vegetables are soft, about 50 minutes, adding more water if needed. Taste and adjust seasonings, if necessary. Remove from heat and stir in the vinegar, if using. Serve hot.

Cincinnati Suburb Chili

Makes 4 servings

Distinctive in its many layers and sweet, aromatic flavor, Cincinnati chili makes a great weeknight meal. The recipe is somewhat on the outskirts of the original, with less layers and no meat or cheese—more like a "suburb" of Cincinnati chili.

1 tablespoon olive oil
2 medium sweet yellow onions, minced
2 garlic cloves, minced
1 (14.5-ounce) can crushed tomatoes
2 tablespoons chili powder
1 tablespoon unsweetened cocoa powder
1 teaspoon sugar
½ teaspoon ground cumin

½ teaspoon ground cinnamon
½ teaspoon ground allspice
½ teaspoon salt
½ teaspoon black pepper
1 cup water
4 cups cooked or 3 (15.5-ounce) cans dark red kidney beans, drained and rinsed
8 ounces spaghetti
Cheezee Sauce (page 36)

1 In a large pot, heat the oil over medium heat. Reserve about ½ cup of the minced onion and set it aside. Add the remaining onion to the pot, cover, and cook until softened, 5 minutes. Add the garlic and cook 1 minute.

2 Stir in the tomatoes, chili powder, cocoa, sugar, cumin, cinnamon, allspice, salt, pepper, and water and bring to a boil. Reduce heat to low, add the beans and simmer for 45 minutes, stirring occasionally.

3 In a large pot of boiling salted water, cook the spaghetti over medium-high heat, stirring occasionally, until al dente, 8 to 10 minutes. Drain well.

4 To serve, layer spaghetti in the bottom of 4 shallow soup bowls, spoon the chili over the spaghetti, and top with the reserved ½ cup minced onion. Drizzle with the cheezee sauce, and serve at once.

Splurge a Little

Sprinkle with shredded vegan cheddar cheese instead of the cheezee sauce.

Satisfying Salads

*A*nyone watching their pennies knows that lettuce can be a pricey commodity. Yet, salads made with lettuces and other fresh ingredients are an important part of a healthy and well-balanced diet. Rather than merely relegating salad greens to a role of an expensive side dish, I like to incorporate them into the main event that, when including with beans, grains, and other ingredients, results in a thrifty one-dish meal in itself.

Another point to remember is that salads don't always need to contain lettuce. Most any vegetable, whether raw or cooked, can be transformed into a salad with a little help from some other ingredients, perhaps another vegetable or two or some beans and a zesty dressing.

The diverse salads in this chapter all share the common bond of being loaded with enough flavorful and nutritious components to make a meal. Flavors of the Southwest prevail in Orange-Chipotle Dressed Salad with Black Bean Salsa (page 87), Nacho Taco Salad (page 94), and Red Bean and Corn Salad (page 95). For sumptuous Asian flavors, try the Peanut Noodle Salad (page 101), Korean Cabbage Salad with Tofu (page 102), or the Tempeh Lettuce Cups (page 100). If you're in the mood for Mediterranean, there's Roasted Root Vegetable Salad with French Lentils and Walnuts (page 88), Tabbouleh Chickpea Salad (page 96), and Skordalia Potato and Green Bean Salad (page 98).

Spend Less on Lettuce

If you want to spend less when buying salad greens, here are some tips:

- Choose whichever lettuce is on sale—sometimes it's red leaf lettuce, other times it's romaine.

- Be sure your lettuce is in good shape—no wilted or bruised leaves. If it's fresh and crisp, it will last longer and you won't have to toss it out, which will save money.

- Stretch the salad dollar by buying a small amount of the more expensive salad greens in bulk and mixing them with a less expensive green to add variety and a taste of luxury.

- Make your lettuce last longer by adding extra inexpensive goodies to your salad. Some grated cabbage or carrot, or thinly sliced celery, for example, adds crunch and nutrients and bulks up the salad so you can stretch your lettuce further.

Garden Rotini and Chickpea Salad with Inner Goddess Dressing

<$1.50 per serving

Makes 4 to 6 servings

I used to serve this salad with a certain delicious but expensive bottled "goddess" dressing. To save money, I summoned my inner goddess and came up with this doppelganger version that makes a great creamy all-around salad dressing as well.

¼ cup unsalted raw cashews

2 green onions, chopped

1 garlic clove, crushed

3 tablespoons chopped fresh parsley

½ cup plain unsweetened soy milk

3 tablespoons tahini (sesame paste)

2 tablespoons apple cider vinegar

1 tablespoon fresh lemon juice

1 tablespoon soy sauce

2 teaspoons olive oil

½ teaspoon salt

8 ounces tricolor rotini

1½ cups cooked or 1 (15-ounce) can chickpeas, drained and rinsed

1 medium carrot, shredded

1 celery rib, chopped

1 cup cherry tomatoes, halved

2 radishes, cut into ¼-inch slices

1 cucumber, peeled, halved, seeded, and cut into ¼-inch slices

½ cup thawed frozen peas

1 In a high-speed blender, grind the cashews to a powder. Add the green onions, garlic, and parsley and pulse to mince. Add the soy milk, tahini, vinegar, lemon juice, soy sauce, oil, and salt, and process until smooth. Set aside.

2 In a large pot of boiling salted water, cook the rotini over medium-high heat, stirring occasionally, until al dente, 8 to 10 minutes. Drain well and transfer to a large bowl. Set aside until cool.

3 Add the chickpeas, carrot, celery, tomatoes, radishes, cucumber, and peas. Drizzle with about half of the dressing and toss gently to combine. Taste and adjust seasonings, adding more of the dressing if desired or reserving it for another use. Serve at once.

Splurge a Little

Add ½ cup halved pitted kalamata olives to the salad.

Curried Vegetable Salad

<$1.50 per serving

Makes 4 to 6 servings

This boldly flavored salad tastes even better once the flavors have time to mingle, so plan to make it a few hours ahead of serving time. You can also vary the vegetables, using sweet potatoes instead of white or swapping in cauliflower or green beans for the broccoli.

½ cup plus 2 tablespoons unsalted roasted cashews

½ cup plain unsweetened soy milk

½ cup Make-Your-Own Mayo (page 41)

1 tablespoon hot or mild curry powder

½ teaspoon salt

1 pound white potatoes, peeled and cut into 1-inch dice

1½ cups small broccoli florets

1½ cups cooked or 1 (14.5-ounce) can chickpeas, drained and rinsed

1 cup thawed frozen peas

1 medium carrot, shredded

½ cup golden raisins or chopped dried apricots

¼ cup minced green onions

❶ In a high-speed blender, grind the ½ cup cashews to a powder. Add the soy milk, mayo, curry powder, and salt and blend until smooth. Set aside.

❷ Steam the potatoes until just tender, 12 to 15 minutes. Transfer to a large bowl and set aside.

❸ Steam the broccoli until just tender, about 5 minutes, and then add to the bowl with the potatoes.

❹ Add the chickpeas, peas, carrot, raisins, and green onions. Add the cashew sauce and mix gently to combine. Taste and adjust seasonings, adding more curry powder or salt, if necessary. Sprinkle with the remaining 2 tablespoons cashews and serve at once, or cover and refrigerate until needed.

Splurge a Little

For convenience, use Vegenaise or another commercial vegan mayonnaise in place of Make-Your-Own Mayo.

Orange-Chipotle Dressed Salad with Black Bean Salsa

<$1.00 per serving

Makes 4 servings

The smoky heat of chipotle chile and the tangy sweetness of oranges combine for a well-dressed salad that is topped with a lively black bean salsa. For a tasty lunchtime treat, serve it accompanied with the Cheapamole on page 35 and a big bowl of tortilla chips.

1 cup cooked or canned black beans, drained and rinsed	1 chipotle chile in adobo
1 small ripe tomato, chopped	1 small ripe tomato, halved
¼ cup minced red onion	2 tablespoons fresh orange juice
2 tablespoons chopped fresh cilantro	2 tablespoons olive oil
2 tablespoons apple cider vinegar	½ teaspoon sugar
Salt	4 to 5 cups salad greens
	2 navel oranges, peeled and sectioned (see Note)

1 In a medium bowl, combine the beans, tomato, onion, cilantro, vinegar, and ¼ teaspoon salt, stirring gently to mix well. Taste and adjust seasonings, if necessary. Set aside or cover and refrigerate until ready to use.

2 In a blender, combine the chile, tomato, orange juice, oil, sugar, and ¼ teaspoon salt and blend until smooth.

3 Place the salad greens in a large bowl. Add about three-quarters of the dressing and toss to combine. To serve, divide the dressed greens among 4 salad plates. Spoon some of the salsa on top and arrange the orange slices decoratively around the salsa. Drizzle with the remaining dressing. Serve at once.

Note: To section oranges, use a small serrated knife to cut the sections out on either side of the membrane, so that just the orange "supremes" remain for the salad.

Splurge a Little

Add a diced ripe avocado to the salad.

Roasted Root Vegetable Salad with French Lentils and Walnuts

<$1.50 per serving

Makes 4 to 6 servings

This sophisticated salad is surprisingly inexpensive to make, and, with protein-rich nutritional powerhouses like lentils, walnuts, and tofu combined with loads of healthful veggies, it's also a terrific one-dish meal. Warm French bread is an ideal accompaniment. Tiny green lentils are used in this recipe because they hold their shape well, but you can substitute brown lentils if you prefer, as long as you do not overcook them.

½ cup French lentils, picked over, rinsed, and drained

2 large beets

2 medium carrots, cut into ¼-inch strips

2 medium parsnips, peeled and cut into ¼-inch strips

Salt and black pepper

⅓ cup olive oil, plus more for roasting vegetables

1½ tablespoons Dijon mustard

1 teaspoon dried marjoram

1 tablespoon chopped fresh parsley

2 tablespoons red wine vinegar

½ teaspon sugar

6 cups mixed salad greens

½ cup Tofeta (page 37)

¼ cup toasted walnuts

1 Bring a large saucepan of salted water to boil over high heat. Add the lentils, return to a boil, then reduce heat to low. Cover and cook until tender, about 40 minutes. Drain and set aside. Preheat the oven to 400°F.

2 Place the beets on a sheet of foil and drizzle with oil. Seal the beets in the foil and roast until soft, about 1 hour. Arrange the carrots and parsnips in a single layer in an oiled baking pan. Drizzle with oil and season with salt and pepper to taste. Cover tightly with foil and roast until soft, 30 to 40 minutes.

3 When the vegetables are tender, remove them from the oven and set aside to cool for about 10 minutes. When the beets are cool enough to handle, remove the skin and then cut them into thin slices and set aside.

4 In a small bowl, combine the mustard, marjoram, parsley, vinegar, sugar, and salt and pepper to taste. Stir in the remaining ⅓ cup of oil and mix until well blended. Taste and adjust seasonings.

5 Toss the lettuce with about one-third of the dressing and arrange on salad plates.

6 In a large bowl, combine the cooked lentils with the tofeta, walnuts, and one-third of the dressing. Spoon the lentil mixture onto the lettuce, dividing evenly.

7 Toss each of the roasted vegetables separately with the remaining dressing and arrange them decoratively on top of the salad. Serve at once.

Bean and Barley Salad with Creamy Dijon Dressing

<$1.00 per serving

Makes 4 servings

Barley is a nutritious and healthful grain that adds a chewy texture to this hearty salad complemented by a creamy mustard dressing. If you don't have raw cashews on hand, roasted unsalted cashews may be substituted.

1 cup pearl barley
½ cup unsalted raw cashews
½ cup water
1 tablespoon Dijon mustard
1 tablespoon soy sauce
1 tablespoon fresh lemon juice
Salt and black pepper
1½ cups cooked or 1 (15.5-ounce)
   can white beans, drained
   and rinsed

2 celery ribs, chopped
2 medium carrots, shredded
2 green onions, minced
Lettuce leaves, for serving
   (optional)

❶ In a large saucepan of boiling salted water, cook the barley until tender, about 45 minutes. Drain and transfer to a large bowl. Set aside to cool.

❷ In a high-speed blender, grind the cashews to a powder. Add the water, mustard, soy sauce, lemon juice, and salt and pepper to taste. Blend until smooth and creamy. Taste and adjust seasonings, if necessary. Transfer to a small bowl and set aside.

❸ To the bowl containing the barley, add the beans, celery, carrots, and green onions. Pour on about half the dressing and toss to combine. Taste and adjust seasonings, adding more dressing, if desired.

❹ Serve as is or spoon onto lettuce leaves that have been arranged on plates and drizzled with some of the remaining dressing.

Pasta Slaw

Makes 4 to 6 servings

What happens when you combine coleslaw and pasta salad? You end up with a delicious "pasta slaw" that has the refreshing crunch of shredded cabbage and carrots and the satisfying chewiness of penne pasta. Bits of apple add a sweet surprise. Although this salad can also be made with a sweet and creamy slaw-type dressing, I think this lighter oil and vinegar dressing does a better job at enhancing the flavor of the other ingredients. Serve with a sandwich or veggie burger for a satisfying meal, or toss in a can of beans or some diced sautéed tempeh or baked tofu and call it dinner.

8 ounces penne	2 tablespoons apple cider vinegar
3 cups shredded cabbage	1 teaspoon sugar
2 medium carrots, shredded	½ teaspoon salt
2 green onions, minced	¼ teaspoon black pepper
½ cup toasted walnut pieces	1 large crisp apple
¼ cup olive oil	

1. In a large pot of boiling salted water, cook the penne over medium-high heat, stirring occasionally, until al dente, about 10 minutes. Drain well and rinse with cold water to stop the cooking process. Transfer the pasta to a large bowl.

2. Add the cabbage, carrots, green onions, and walnuts to the bowl containing the pasta. Set aside.

3. In a small bowl, combine the oil, vinegar, sugar, salt, and pepper. Mix until well blended. Set aside.

4. Core the apple and cut it into ¼-inch strips. Add the apple to the pasta and cabbage mixture and pour on the dressing. Toss until well combined. Serve at once.

Splurge a Little

Choose a Braeburn or Gala apple for the salad. They are sometimes a bit costlier than other varieties but have a wonderful flavor and crisp texture.

Roasted Sweet Potato Salad with Cashews and Kidney Beans

<$1.00 per serving

Makes 4 servings

If it's true that we first eat with our eyes, then you'll gobble up this gorgeous salad as soon as you see it. The wonderful color combination is just a hint of the marvelous flavors and textures in store. If you've never had roasted sweet potatoes in a salad, you owe it to yourself to give them a try. The dressing can be enjoyed on other salads as well.

Dressing
2 tablespoons white wine vinegar
1 teaspoon grated fresh ginger
½ teaspoon Dijon mustard
2 tablespoons chopped fresh
  cilantro or parsley
1 teaspoon sugar
1 teaspoon salt
⅛ teaspoon ground cayenne
¼ cup olive oil

Salad
2 medium sweet potatoes
Salt and black pepper
Olive oil
¼ cup minced green onions
1½ cups cooked or 1 (15.5-ounce)
  can dark red kidney beans,
  drained and rinsed
⅔ cup thawed frozen peas
¼ cup roasted unsalted cashews,
  coarsely chopped
4 cups salad greens

❶ Make the dressing: In a small bowl, combine the vinegar, ginger, mustard, cilantro, sugar, salt, and cayenne. Stir in the oil until well blended. Set aside.

❷ Make the salad: Preheat the oven to 400°F. Lightly oil a baking sheet and set aside. Peel the sweet potatoes, cut into ½-inch dice, and arrange on the prepared baking sheet. Season with salt and pepper to taste and drizzle with olive oil. Roast the potatoes until tender, about 20 minutes, turning once halfway through. Remove from the oven and set aside to cool.

❸ In a large bowl, combine the green onions, beans, peas, cashews, and cooked sweet potatoes. Add about half of the dressing and toss to combine.

④ Place the salad greens in a large bowl. Add the remaining dressing and toss to coat.

⑤ To serve, divide the dressed greens among 4 salad plates and top with the sweet potato salad.

Variation

Omit the salad greens and serve as a side dish instead of a salad.

Nacho Taco Salad

<$1.50 per serving

Makes 4 to 6 servings

If you're looking for a salad that's economical, fun to eat, and a big hit with older children and teenagers, this is it.

1½ cups cooked or 1 (15.5-ounce) can black beans, drained and rinsed

1½ cups cooked or 1 (15.5-ounce) can pinto beans, drained and rinsed

2 cups Salsa in Season (page 34)

2 teaspoons chili powder

1 cup Cheezee Sauce (page 36)

4 cups tortilla chips

3 cups shredded iceberg lettuce

2 ripe plum tomatoes, diced

Optional toppings: sliced pitted black olives, canned chopped mild or hot green chiles, Cheapamole (page 35)

1 In a large saucepan, combine the black beans, pinto beans, 1 cup of the salsa, and the chili powder. Use a fork to mash a portion of the beans. Cook over medium heat, stirring occasionally to heat through, for 5 to 7 minutes. Keep warm.

2 In a small saucepan, heat the cheezee sauce and keep warm.

3 To serve, divide the tortilla chips among plates or shallow bowls. Spoon the bean mixture over the chips. Drizzle with the cheezee sauce. Sprinkle on the lettuce and tomato and serve at once, passing the remaining salsa and any desired toppings at the table.

Splurge a Little

Serve with regular guacamole made with avocados. Sprinkle with shredded vegan cheddar cheese instead of using the cheezee sauce.

Red Bean and Corn Salad

< 50¢
per serving

Makes 4 to 6 servings

This colorful salad is easy to make and can be assembled ahead of when you need it. To stretch it further and make it a meal, add 2 cups of cold cooked rice and toss to combine.

3 cups cooked or 2 (15.5-ounce) cans dark red kidney beans, drained and rinsed

2 cups thawed frozen corn kernels

½ cup sliced celery

¼ cup minced red onion

¼ cup chopped fresh parsley or cilantro

2½ tablespoons apple cider vinegar

1 teaspoon sugar

¼ cup olive oil

¼ teaspoon salt

Black pepper

❶ In a large bowl, combine the beans, corn, celery, onion, and parsley. Set aside.

❷ In a small bowl, combine the vinegar, sugar, oil, salt, and a few generous grindings of pepper to taste. Mix until blended.

❸ Pour the dressing onto the salad and stir to mix well. Serve at once.

Splurge a Little

Top with diced avocado.

Tabbouleh Chickpea Salad

<$1.00 per serving

Makes 4 to 6 servings

Since bulgur comes already steamed and dried, it only requires soaking rather than cooking for a soft, fluffy grain. Serve over lettuce accompanied by warm pita and the Handy Hummus on page 44.

1 cup bulgur
Salt
2 cups boiling water
1 cup minced fresh parsley
½ small red onion, minced
1 medium ripe tomato, chopped

1½ cups cooked or 1 (15.5-ounce) can chickpeas, drained and rinsed
¼ cup olive oil
2 tablespoons white wine vinegar
Black pepper

1 Place the bulgur and ¼ teaspoon of salt in a heatproof bowl. Stir in the water and set aside for 20 to 30 minutes, or until the liquid is absorbed.

2 Squeeze out any remaining liquid from the bulgur and transfer it to a large bowl. Add the parsley, onion, tomato, and chickpeas.

3 Add the oil and vinegar, and season with salt and pepper to taste. Mix well, then taste and adjust the seasonings, if necessary, and serve.

Splurge a Little

Use fresh lemon juice instead of vinegar. Add halved pitted kalamata olives.

Thai-Style Pineapple Rice Salad

<$1.00 per serving

Makes 4 to 6 servings

Fragrant jasmine rice and pineapple are complemented by a spicy sweet dressing. Serve it as is on a bed of lettuce or turn it into a satisfying one-dish meal by adding diced baked tofu and your choice of blanched snow peas, thawed frozen green peas, or steamed broccoli florets. The next time you make rice, plan ahead and make extra for this salad. If you don't have jasmine rice, another variety may be used.

3 cups cold cooked jasmine rice

1½ cups chopped fresh or canned pineapple, drained

1 large carrot, shredded

½ cup thawed frozen green peas

¼ cup minced green onions

1 small hot red chile, seeded and minced

½ cup chopped fresh cilantro

¼ cup chopped unsalted roasted peanuts

¼ cup rice vinegar

3 tablespoons soy sauce

1 tablespoon toasted sesame oil

2 teaspoons light brown sugar

¼ teaspoon salt

1 In a large bowl, combine the rice, pineapple, carrot, peas, green onions, chile, cilantro, and peanuts. Set aside.

2 In a small bowl, combine the vinegar, soy sauce, oil, sugar, and salt, stirring to dissolve.

3 Pour the dressing over the salad and toss to combine. Serve at once or cover and refrigerate until needed and serve chilled.

Skordalia Potato and Green Bean Salad

<$1.00 per serving

Makes 4 to 6 servings

This delicious potato salad owes much of its great flavor to skordalia, a garlicky Greek aioli-type sauce made with potatoes. If you have imported olives in the house (or want to splurge a little), they make a wonderful addition to the salad, as do capers (use them if you've got them). This salad is also great with the addition of chopped fresh dill or basil, if you have some on hand. I like to leave the peels on the potatoes (scrubbed well), although you can peel them if you prefer.

1 pound Yukon Gold or other white potatoes, unpeeled, cut into ½-inch dice

12 ounces green beans, trimmed and cut into 1-inch pieces

1 large ripe tomato, diced

2 tablespoons minced red onion

¼ cup chopped fresh parsley

1¼ cups Skordalia (recipe follows)

Salt and black pepper

1. Steam the potatoes until just tender, 12 to 15 minutes. Transfer to a large bowl.

2. Steam the green beans until just tender, 8 to 10 minutes. Run under cold water to stop the cooking process, then drain well, and add to the bowl with the potatoes.

3. To the same bowl, add the tomato, onion, and parsley. Add the skordalia and season with salt and pepper to taste. Toss gently to combine.

4. Taste and adjust seasonings, if necessary. Serve immediately.

Splurge a Little

Add halved pitted kalamata olives and/or capers.

Skordalia

Makes about 2 cups

Similar to aioli, but thickened with bread or nuts, this creamy Greek garlic sauce makes a great alternative to mayonnaise in potato salad. It can also be drizzled over roasted vegetables or cooked grains or used as a topping for veggie burgers.

1 large russet potato, peeled and cut into ½-inch dice

¼ cup plain unsweetened soy milk

3 garlic cloves

2 slices white bread, crusts removed and cut into ½-inch dice

3 tablespoons fresh lemon juice

⅓ cup olive oil

¾ teaspoon salt

➊ Steam the potato until just tender, about 12 minutes, then transfer to a large bowl. Add the soy milk and mash well. Set aside.

➋ Run the garlic through a press, then add to the mashed potato and mix well to combine.

➌ In a medium bowl, soak the bread cubes in enough water to cover until softened. Squeeze out the water and discard. Mash the bread with a fork and stir into the potato mixture.

➍ Stir in the lemon juice, then slowly add the oil in a steady stream, stirring until thick and creamy. Stir in the salt. Cover and refrigerate until needed. Properly stored, the sauce will keep well for 3 to 4 days.

Tempeh Lettuce Cups

<$2.00 per serving

Makes 4 to 6 servings

This salad is a great way to introduce tempeh to the table. Not only is it loaded with great flavors, but it's fun to eat, too. It also features iceberg lettuce, which is often less expensive than other varieties.

8 ounces tempeh

2 tablespoons light brown sugar

½ cup water

¼ cup soy sauce

2 tablespoons rice vinegar

2 tablespoons hoisin sauce

1 tablespoon fresh lemon juice

1 to 2 teaspoons Asian chili paste

2 teaspoons toasted sesame oil

2 tablespoons canola or other
　　neutral oil

¼ cup chopped onion

1 teaspoon minced garlic

1 cup minced white mushrooms

1 cup minced water chestnuts

8 to 12 whole leaves iceberg lettuce

1 In a medium saucepan of simmering water, cook the tempeh over medium heat for 30 minutes. Drain, pat dry, and set aside to cool.

2 In a small bowl, combine the sugar, water, soy sauce, vinegar, hoisin sauce, lemon juice, chili paste, and sesame oil. Mix well and set aside.

3 In a large skillet or wok, heat the canola oil over medium-high heat. Crumble the cooked tempeh and add it to the skillet. Cook, stirring, until browned, about 5 minutes. Remove the tempeh from the skillet and set aside.

4 To the same skillet, add the onion and garlic, and cook until softened, about 5 minutes. Stir in the mushrooms and water chestnuts and cook 2 minutes longer. Add the cooked tempeh and the prepared sauce. Simmer, stirring, for 3 to 5 minutes to blend the flavors.

5 To serve, spoon the tempeh mixture into the lettuce leaves.

Peanut Noodle Salad

<$2.00
per serving

Makes 4 servings

Packaged baked tofu and bottled peanut sauce can be expensive. Cut the cost and make your own to use in this scrumptious salad that only tastes like a luxury.

1 pound extra-firm tofu, drained
   and patted dry
¼ cup soy sauce
8 ounces linguine
2 teaspoons toasted sesame oil
4 green onions, minced

1 large carrot, shredded
1 medium red bell pepper, cut into
   matchsticks
3 cups broccoli florets, steamed
Easy Peanut Sauce (page 40)

1 Preheat the oven to 375°F. Lightly oil a baking sheet and set aside.

2 Cut the tofu into ½-inch slabs and press well to remove any excess water. Cut the slabs into ½-inch cubes and toss with the soy sauce. Arrange the tofu on the prepared baking sheet and bake for 30 minutes. Remove from the oven and set aside to cool.

3 In a large pot of boiling salted water, cook the linguine over medium-high heat, stirring occasionally, until al dente, about 10 minutes. Drain and rinse under cold water. Transfer to a large bowl and toss with the oil.

4 Add the green onions, carrot, bell pepper, and steamed broccoli to the noodles. Pour on enough peanut sauce to coat and toss gently to combine. Serve topped with the baked tofu.

Splurge a Little

For convenience, use store-bought baked marinated tofu and bottled peanut sauce.

Korean Cabbage Salad with Tofu

<$1.50 per serving

Makes 4 servings

This refreshing and tangy cabbage salad teams with bake-your-own tofu for a delicious and healthful meal that doesn't break the bank.

1 pound extra-firm tofu, drained
    and patted dry
½ cup soy sauce
5 cups shredded cabbage
2 medium carrots, shredded
3 green onions, minced
2 garlic cloves, minced

1 tablespoon minced fresh ginger
1 tablespoon light brown sugar
1 teaspoon Asian chili paste
¼ cup rice vinegar
3 tablespoons toasted sesame oil
3 tablespoons water

1 Preheat the oven to 375°F. Lightly oil a baking sheet and set aside.

2 Cut the tofu into ½-inch slabs and press well to remove any excess water. Cut the slabs into ½-inch cubes and toss with ¼ cup of the soy sauce. Arrange the tofu on the prepared baking sheet and bake for 30 minutes. Remove from the oven and set aside to cool.

3 In a large bowl, combine the cabbage, carrots, and green onions. Set aside.

4 In a small bowl, combine the garlic, ginger, sugar, chili paste, remaining ¼ cup soy sauce, vinegar, oil, and water.

5 Pour the dressing over the cabbage mixture and toss to combine. Taste and adjust seasonings, if necessary. Let the salad to sit for 15 to 20 minutes to allow flavors to develop. Serve topped with the tofu.

Noodle Know-How

I grew up in a home where thrifty meals were a way of life, and nothing was ever wasted. Not surprisingly, pasta dishes were often on my family's menu two to three times a week and they were always our favorite meals.

Cooks today realize the virtues of pasta just as my mother and grandmother did. It's inexpensive, satisfying, easy to prepare, and versatile. Pasta is also generally enjoyed even by finicky eaters, making it a reliable choice for stress-free dining when there are children in the house.

While there are luxurious exceptions (think truffle sauce), pasta and noodle dishes are generally one of the most economical ways to enjoy a satisfying meal and not feel like you're pinching pennies.

If you're tired of the same spaghetti with tomato sauce, let recipes such as Walnut-Dusted Fettuccine with Caramelized Vegetables (page 120), Fusilli with Potatoes, Green Beans, and Lemon Basil Crème (page 119), and Dan Dan–Style Linguine (page 124) show you ways to enjoy scrumptious dishes that taste anything but budget-conscious.

Linguine with Variations on a Pesto

<$1.50 per serving

Makes 4 servings

Traditional pesto calls for fresh basil. Pesto lovers know that buying basil can be expensive, so the best defense is to grow your own—even in a pot on the windowsill. I grow lots of basil in my summer garden so I can make enough pesto to freeze in batches to get me through the winter. I have yet to find a truly economical source for the classic pine nuts found in pesto, so I usually substitute another nut in its place, with delicious results. The optional nutritional yeast adds a salty-cheesy flavor to the pesto.

3 garlic cloves
¼ cup slivered almonds, lightly toasted
½ teaspoon salt
2 cups firmly packed fresh basil leaves

2 tablespoons nutritional yeast (optional)
2 teaspoons fresh lemon juice
Black pepper
¼ cup olive oil
1 pound linguine

1 In a food processor, combine the garlic, almonds, and salt and process until finely minced. Add the basil, yeast, if using, lemon juice, and pepper to taste. Process to a paste. With the machine running, stream in the oil until combined. Set aside.

2 In a large pot of boiling salted water, cook the linguine over medium-high heat, stirring occasionally, until al dente, about 10 minutes. Drain, reserving about ½ cup of the cooking water, and return the linguine to the pot. Add as much of the pesto as desired and the reserved cooking water and toss to coat. Serve hot with a few grindings of black pepper.

Variations

Stretching the Basil: If you find yourself with just a small amount of basil, you can still make a great pesto. Simply put your basil leaves in a 2-cup measure and add parsley and spinach leaves to make up the difference. Then proceed with the recipe.

Basil-Free Pesto: Sometimes the pesto supply in my freezer runs out in mid-February, which is when I rely on my favorite wintertime pesto made with spinach and walnuts. To make this variation, simply substitute spinach leaves for the basil and toasted walnut pieces for the almonds, then proceed with the recipe.

Splurge a Little

Use pine nuts instead of almonds or walnuts.

Blushing Alfredo Fettuccine

<$1.50 per serving

Makes 4 servings

Enjoy this creamy and flavorful pasta as is or use it as a jumping-off point for several variations: Omit the marinara sauce for a more traditional-style Alfredo sauce; add 2 cups bite-size cooked veggies for a creamy primavera; top with sautéed sliced almonds and green beans; top with diced baked tempeh or tofu chunks; stir in some sautéed spinach or other leafy greens.

1 tablespoon olive oil
1 small yellow onion, chopped
3 garlic cloves, minced
2 tablespoons dry white wine
⅓ cup unsalted raw cashews
½ cup silken tofu, drained
2 tablespoons nutritional yeast

1½ cups plain unsweetened soy milk
½ cup Marinara Sauce (page 32)
½ teaspoon salt
1 pound fettuccine
2 tablespoons minced fresh parsley
Black pepper

1 In a medium saucepan, heat the oil over medium heat. Add the onion and garlic, cover, and cook until soft, about 5 minutes. Stir in the wine, remove from heat, and set aside.

2 In a high-speed blender, grind the cashews to a powder. Add the onion-garlic mixture, tofu, and yeast and process until smooth. Add the soy milk, marinara sauce, and salt, and blend until smooth. Transfer to the saucepan with the onion-garlic mixture and heat over low heat, stirring occasionally. Keep warm.

3 In a large pot of boiling salted water, cook the fettuccine over medium-high heat, stirring occasionally, until al dente, about 10 minutes. Drain the pasta and return it to the pot. Toss with the sauce. Taste and adjust the seasonings, if necessary. Serve sprinkled with the parsley and a few grindings of black pepper.

Splurge a Little

Use vegan cream cheese instead of tofu for a richer flavor.

Rotini with Spicy Vegetable Ragu

<$2.00 per serving

Makes 4 servings

Red and yellow peppers are sweeter than the green ones (and more vibrantly colored as well), but green bell peppers are usually less expensive. Economical solutions abound: When colored bells are on sale, buy several, cut them into strips and freeze them; look for frozen multicolored bell pepper strips on sale; grow your own bell peppers and freeze or jar them for year-round enjoyment.

1 pound rotini	1 (28-ounce) can diced tomatoes,
3 tablespoons olive oil	drained
4 ounces Big Stick Pepperoni (page	2 tablespoons chopped fresh basil
56), chopped	or parsley
1 medium red onion, chopped	½ teaspoon crushed red pepper
1 large green bell pepper, chopped	(optional)
2 small zucchini, halved lengthwise	1 teaspoon salt
and cut into ¼-inch slices	Black pepper
3 garlic cloves	

❶ In a large pot of boiling salted water, cook the rotini over medium-high heat, stirring occasionally, until al dente, about 10 minutes.

❷ While the pasta is cooking, heat 1 tablespoon of the oil in a large skillet over medium heat. Add the pepperoni and cook for 1 minute. Remove from the skillet with a slotted spoon and set aside.

❸ Heat the remaining oil in the same skillet over medium heat. Add the onion, bell pepper, zucchini, and garlic. Cover and cook, stirring occasionally, until soft, about 10 minutes. Stir in the tomatoes, basil, crushed red pepper, if using, salt, and several grindings of black pepper. Simmer to allow flavors to blend and to break up the tomatoes, about 5 minutes.

❹ When the pasta is cooked, drain well and return it to the pot. Add the sauce and the cooked pepperoni to the pasta and toss to combine. Serve hot.

Splurge a Little

Dice some canned or cooked frozen artichoke hearts and add to the sauce. Use a red or yellow bell pepper instead of a green one.

Spaghetti Marinara with Wheatballs

<$2.00 per serving

Makes 4 servings

Spaghetti and meatballs is the quintessential pasta dish, and this recipe makes it happen vegan-style by using wheat instead of meat in the meatballs. It saves money, too, since packaged vegan meatballs are very expensive. The rich marinara sauce can be served without the wheatballs and can be used anytime you need a good tomato sauce. Instead of the wheatballs, you can add chopped-up seitan or veggie burgers for a tasty "meat" sauce.

2 tablespoons olive oil	1 teaspoon sugar
1 small yellow onion, chopped	1 teaspoon salt
1 celery rib, minced	¼ teaspoon black pepper
2 medium carrots, chopped	2 bay leaves
3 garlic cloves, minced	1 (28-ounce) can crushed tomatoes
1 (6-ounce) can tomato paste	12 ounces spaghetti
¾ teaspoon dried oregano	12 Wheatballs (page 57), hot
¾ teaspoon dried basil	

1 In a large saucepan, heat the oil over medium heat. Add the onion, celery, carrots, and garlic. Cover and cook until the vegetables are soft, about 10 minutes. Stir in the tomato paste, oregano, basil, sugar, salt, pepper, and bay leaves. Cook, stirring, for 3 minutes. Add the crushed tomatoes and simmer uncovered over low heat until the sauce thickens, about 45 minutes.

2 Remove the sauce from the heat and let it cool slightly. Remove and discard the bay leaves. Use an immersion blender to puree the solids in the sauce, or scoop the solids into a blender or food processor and blend until smooth, then return it to the pot. Set aside half of the sauce and return the remaining sauce to the stove and reheat over medium heat for 10 minutes.

3 In a large pot of boiling salted water, cook the spaghetti over medium-high heat, stirring occasionally, until al dente, about 10 minutes. Drain well and divide among 4 plates or shallow bowls.

❹ Make sure the wheatballs are hot, either by sauteing in a skillet for a few minutes or heating in the oven. To serve, top each serving of pasta with 3 wheatballs. Ladle the hot sauce over the pasta and wheatballs and serve at once. Store remaining sauce in a tightly covered container in the refrigerator or freezer. Properly stored, the sauce will keep for up to 4 days in the refrigerator or 1 to 2 months in the freezer.

Variation

Instead of wheatballs, saute some sliced mushrooms and add to the sauce.

Radiatore with Escarole and White Beans

Makes 4 servings

To save pot-washing time, I use the same pot for all three steps: Cook the greens, cook the pasta, then let the pasta sit in the colander while you heat the oil in the same pot. If escarole is unavailable, substitute curly endive (chicory) or kale. Tender, quick-cooking greens such as spinach or chard may also be used, but they just require a light blanching before chopping for the recipe.

1 medium head escarole

1 pound radiatore or other bite-size pasta

3 tablespoons olive oil

3 garlic cloves, minced

¼ to ½ teaspoon crushed red pepper

1½ cups cooked or 1 (15.5-ounce) can white beans, drained and rinsed

Salt and black pepper

1 In a large pot of boiling salted water, cook the escarole over medium-high heat until tender, about 10 minutes. Drain well, then coarsely chop and set aside.

2 In a large pot of boiling salted water, cook the radiatore over medium-high heat, stirring occasionally until al dente, about 10 minutes. Drain well, drizzle with 1 tablespoon of the oil, and toss to coat. Set aside.

3 In a large pot, heat the remaining 2 tablespoons oil over medium heat. Add the garlic and cook until fragrant, 30 seconds. Stir in the crushed red pepper, beans, and cooked escarole and season with salt and black pepper to taste. Add the cooked pasta and toss gently to combine and heat through. Add a few tablespoons of water or a little more oil, if necessary, to coat the pasta. Add a few more grinds of black pepper and serve hot.

Ziti with Green Olives, White Beans, and Oven-Dried Tomatoes

$1.50 per serving

Makes 4 servings

The creaminess of white beans pairs with the piquancy of green olives, while strips of dried tomatoes add color and richness to this quick and easy sauce. Although imported green olives can be expensive, the less expensive variety found in jars on supermarket shelves works fine for this recipe. As a variation, you can puree the sauce in a blender, adding a little vegetable stock if needed, to make a smooth sauce.

1 pound ziti

2 tablespoons olive oil

3 garlic cloves, minced

1½ cups cooked or 1 (15.5-ounce) can white beans, drained and rinsed

1 (14.5-ounce) can diced tomatoes, drained

½ cup sliced pitted green olives

½ cup Oven-Dried Tomatoes (page 33), cut into ⅛-inch strips

¼ cup minced fresh parsley

Salt and black pepper

❶ In a large pot of boiling salted water, cook the ziti over medium-high heat, stirring occasionally, until al dente, about 10 minutes.

❷ While the pasta is cooking, heat the oil in a large skillet over medium heat. Add the garlic and cook, stirring, until softened, about 1 minute. Do not burn. Stir in the beans, canned tomatoes, olives, dried tomatoes, and parsley. Season with salt and pepper to taste.

❸ When the pasta is cooked, drain well and return to the pot. Add the sauce and toss to combine. Serve hot.

Splurge a Little

Add a tablespoon of capers when you add the olives. Use more expensive imported green olives. Use bottled sun-dried tomatoes packed in oil.

Linguine with Lentils and Roasted Butternut Squash

<$1.50 per serving

Makes 4 servings

Roasted squash and fragrant sage transform this supremely economical dish into a sophisticated dish worthy of serving to guests.

½ cup brown lentils, picked over, rinsed, and drained

1 medium butternut squash, peeled, halved, and seeded

Salt and black pepper

2 tablespoons olive oil, plus more for roasting squash

½ cup minced yellow onion

4 garlic cloves, minced

2 teaspoons crumbled dried sage

1 (14.5-ounce) can diced tomatoes, undrained

1 cup vegetable stock (page 45)

12 ounces linguine

❶ Bring a medium saucepan of salted water to boil over high heat. Add the lentils, return to a boil, then reduce heat to low. Cover and cook until tender, about 45 minutes. Drain and set aside.

❷ Preheat the oven to 400°F. Lightly oil a 9 × 13-inch baking pan and set aside. Cut the squash into ½-inch dice (you should have about 4 cups of diced squash) and spread in the prepared pan in a single layer. Drizzle with a small amount of oil and season with salt and pepper to taste. Roast until tender, turning once halfway through, about 30 minutes. Set aside.

❸ In a large skillet heat the oil over medium heat. Add the onion, cover, and cook until softened, about 5 minutes. Add the garlic and cook until fragrant, about 30 seconds. Stir in the sage, tomatoes, and the cooked lentils. Stir in the stock and season with salt and pepper to taste. Simmer to blend the flavors, about 5 minutes. (For a creamier sauce, use an immersion blender to blend a portion of the lentil mixture.) Stir in the roasted squash and keep warm over low heat, adding a bit more broth or water if needed for a more saucelike texture.

❹ In a large pot of boiling salted water, cook the linguine over medium-high heat, stirring occasionally, until al dente, about 10 minutes. Drain the pasta and return to the pot. Add the lentil-squash mixture and toss gently to combine. Serve hot.

Splurge a Little

Use fresh sage instead of dried. Use green lentils instead of brown. Add 2 to 3 cups of chopped arugula when you add the garlic.

The Incredible Shrinking Pasta Box

At one time, it seemed that all dried pasta was sold in one-pound boxes. These days, they can range anywhere from eight ounces to seventeen ounces. Most of these recipes call for a pound of pasta, allowing four generous four-ounce servings. But don't worry. If your box has only twelve ounces of pasta, that will work, too; everyone just gets a little less. If, on the other hand, there are just two or three of you and you have a sixteen-ounce box of pasta, I say cook the whole box and just use what you need, saving the rest for another meal. A few ounces of leftover pasta can be transformed into many amazing dishes. It is a great way to stretch soups and stews, or add to a salad or stir-fry. You can never cook up too much pasta!

Farfalle with White Beans and Cabbage

<$1.00 per serving

Makes 4 servings

This is a variation of the economical and delicious Eastern European comfort food dish called *halushki*. The traditional recipe does not contain beans, but I like to add them for a more substantial one-dish meal. If you prefer a dish with more color and a little extra oomph, add any of these additions as a variation: ⅓ cup slivered oven-dried tomatoes or sautéed chopped red bell pepper (for color); 1 tablespoon soy sauce, 1 tablespoon sherry vinegar, 1 teaspoon crumbled dried sage, ¼ teaspoon crushed red pepper (for extra flavor); or top with some green onions for a bit of both.

12 ounces farfalle or other small
    shaped pasta
2 tablespoons extra-virgin olive oil
2 tablespoons vegan margarine
1 large sweet yellow onion,
    chopped
1 small head green cabbage, finely
    shredded (4 to 5 cups)

Salt and black pepper
1½ cups cooked or 1 (15.5-ounce)
    can cannellini beans, drained
    and rinsed
2 tablespoons minced fresh
    parsley

❶ In a large pot of boiling salted water, cook the farfalle over medium-high heat, stirring occasionally, until al dente, 8 to 10 minutes. Drain well and return it to the pot. Set aside.

❷ In a large skillet, heat the oil and margarine over medium heat. Add the onion and cook, stirring, until softened and browned, about 12 minutes. Stir in the cabbage and season well with salt and pepper to taste. Cook, stirring occasionally, until lightly browned, about 10 minutes. Reduce the heat to medium-low and cover the skillet. Continue to cook until the cabbage is soft, about 5 more minutes. Stir in the beans and cook until heated through, about 3 more minutes.

❸ Add the cabbage mixture and parsley to the cooked pasta and toss well to combine, adding more salt and pepper if necessary. Serve hot.

Orzo Pilaf with Tofu Feta

<$2.00 per serving

Makes 4 servings

This recipe is ideal for variations: Use a different pasta shape to replace the orzo; add some cooked chopped broccoli instead of spinach; drizzle with a spritz of fresh lemon juice when ready to serve to make it more piquant.

8 ounces orzo	½ teaspoon dried basil
2 tablespoons olive oil	1½ cups cooked or 1 (15.5-ounce)
1 medium red onion, chopped	can chickpeas, drained and
3 garlic cloves, minced	rinsed
6 ounces fresh spinach, chopped	⅓ cup pitted kalamata olives, sliced
1 (14.5-ounce) can diced tomatoes,	3 tablespoons minced fresh parsley
drained	1 recipe Tofeta, crumbled
½ teaspoon dried oregano	(page 37)

1 In a large pot of boiling salted water, cook the orzo over medium-high heat, stirring occasionally, until al dente, 5 to 7 minutes. Drain and set aside.

2 In a large skillet, heat the oil over medium heat. Add the onion, cover, and cook until softened, about 5 minutes. Stir in the garlic and cook for 30 seconds to soften. Add the spinach and cook, stirring, until wilted. Add the tomatoes, oregano, and basil, and simmer for 1 minute.

3 Stir in the chickpeas, olives, parsley, and cooked orzo and cook until heated through, about 5 minutes. Top with tofeta and serve hot.

Splurge a Little

Add a cup of diced artichoke hearts (canned, drained or frozen, cooked—not the marinated kind). Add extra kalamata olives. Use roasted asparagus (cut into 1-inch pieces) instead of spinach.

Penne and Broccoli with Tomatoes, Walnuts, and Raisins

<$1.00 per serving

Makes 4 servings

All that's missing from this classic Sicilian dish are the anchovies, but most people don't seem to mind that omission. What many people do like about this dish is the variety of delicious flavors and textures, along with the tremendously healthful ingredients: Broccoli is loaded with calcium and vitamin C, and nutrient-rich walnuts are a good source of alpha-linolenic acid, an essential omega-3 fatty acid. If you have fresh herbs on hand, use them instead of dried.

1 pound broccoli, cut into ½-inch florets (4 cups)
1 pound penne
3 tablespoons olive oil
4 garlic cloves, minced
⅓ cup toasted walnut pieces
⅓ cup raisins
¼ cup minced fresh parsley
1 teaspoon dried basil

1 teaspoon dried marjoram
Salt and black pepper
1 (14.5-ounce) can diced tomatoes, undrained
1 (14.5-ounce) can crushed tomatoes
½ teaspoon sugar

1 Steam or blanch the broccoli until just tender, 4 to 5 minutes. Drain, run under cold water to stop the cooking process, and set aside.

2 In a large pot of boiling salted water, cook the penne over medium-high heat, stirring occasionally, until al dente, about 10 minutes.

3 While the pasta is cooking, heat the oil in a large skillet over medium heat. Add the garlic and cook until softened and fragrant, about 1 minute. Do not burn. Add the walnuts, raisins, parsley, basil, marjoram, and salt and pepper to taste. Stir in the diced tomatoes with their juice, crushed tomatoes, and sugar and simmer until the liquid reduces slightly. Add the cooked broccoli and toss to heat through.

4 When the pasta is cooked, drain well and return to the pot. Add the broccoli mixture and toss gently to combine. Serve hot.

Fusilli with Potatoes, Green Beans, and Lemon Basil Crème

<$1.50 per serving

Makes 4 servings

There are a number of Italian dishes that pair potatoes with pasta, including a classic from Genoa that also features green beans and pesto. This recipe is inspired by that dish, offering a creamy basil-infused lemon sauce in place of the pesto. If fusilli is unavailable, substitute another spiral pasta, such as rotini.

1 pound white potatoes, peeled and cut into ½-inch dice

1½ cups green beans, trimmed and cut into 1-inch pieces

12 ounces fusilli

½ cup unsalted raw cashews

2 garlic cloves, crushed

¼ cup water

3 tablespoons fresh lemon juice

2 tablespoons olive oil

1 teaspoon finely grated lemon zest

1 tablespoon nutritional yeast

1 teaspoon dried basil

½ teaspoon onion powder

½ teaspoon salt

1¼ cups plain unsweetened soy milk

3 tablespoons minced fresh basil

1 Steam the potatoes for 5 minutes. Add the green beans and steam until the potatoes and green beans are just tender, 8 to 10 minutes. Run under cold water to stop the cooking process and set aside.

2 In a large pot of boiling salted water, cook the fusilli over medium-high heat, stirring occasionally, until al dente, about 10 minutes.

3 While the pasta is cooking, grind the cashews to a powder in a high-speed blender. Add the garlic, water, lemon juice, oil, zest, yeast, dried basil, onion powder, salt, and soy milk, and blend until smooth. Taste and adjust seasonings, if necessary. Add an additional tablespoon or two of water if the sauce is too thick. Set aside.

4 When the pasta is cooked, drain well and return it to the pot. Add the steamed green beans and potatoes. Add the sauce and the fresh basil, and toss gently to combine. Taste and adjust the seasonings, if necessary. Serve hot.

Walnut-Dusted Fettuccine with Caramelized Vegetables

<$2.00 per serving

Makes 4 servings

Caramelizing the vegetables adds a savory-sweet richness to this chunky sauce. I like to serve it over fettuccine, but a short sturdy pasta shape such as penne works nicely as well. A dusting of ground walnuts contributes a rich finish to the dish.

3 tablespoons olive oil

1 medium sweet yellow onion, chopped

3 garlic cloves, chopped

1 teaspoon dried thyme

½ teaspoon dried savory

½ teaspoon salt

¼ teaspoon black pepper

⅓ cup apple cider vinegar

⅓ cup light brown sugar

1 cup vegetable stock (page 45)

1 medium green bell pepper, diced

1 medium butternut squash, peeled, halved, seeded, and cut into ½-inch dice

8 ounces white mushrooms, lightly rinsed, patted dry, and halved or quartered depending on size

1 pound fettuccine

2 tablespoons minced fresh parsley

⅓ cup ground toasted walnuts

1 In a large skillet, heat 2 tablespoons of the oil over medium heat. Add the onion. Cover and cook until softened, about 5 minutes. Stir in the garlic, thyme, savory, salt, and black pepper. Reduce heat to low. Stir in the vinegar and sugar and simmer, stirring to blend the flavors and dissolve the sugar, about 5 minutes. Add the stock, bell pepper, and squash. Cover and cook until softened, stirring occasionally, about 15 minutes. Stir the mushrooms into the vegetables and simmer until all the vegetables are tender, about 5 minutes longer. Keep covered and warm over low heat.

2 While the vegetables are cooking, cook the fettuccine in a large pot of boiling salted water over medium-high heat, stirring occasionally, until al dente, about 10 minutes. Drain well and return it to the pot. Toss with the vegetable mixture and the remaining 1 tablespoon oil. Sprinkle with the parsley and walnuts and serve hot.

Variations

Substitute diced sweet potatoes for the butternut squash. Stir 2 cups of chopped steamed broccoli florets or roasted halved Brussels sprouts into the finished dish just before serving for added color.

Splurge a Little

Toss the pasta with a couple tablespoons of walnut oil before adding the sauce.

Penne-Wise Peanutty Pasta

<$1.50 per serving

Makes 4 servings

Here's a great way to get a delicious dinner on the table in a few minutes that the whole family will love. (Just omit the crushed red pepper if you have young children.)

2 garlic cloves, crushed

2 green onions, chopped

2 teaspoons grated fresh ginger

4 ounces silken tofu, drained

⅓ cup creamy peanut butter

¼ cup soy sauce

2 tablespoons rice vinegar

1 tablespoon toasted sesame oil

1 tablespoon ketchup

2 tablespoons light brown sugar

½ teaspoon crushed red pepper (optional)

1½ cups plain unsweetened soy milk

12 ounces penne

2 medium carrots, cut into ⅛-inch slices

2 cups small broccoli florets

2 tablespoons minced fresh parsley or cilantro

¼ cup crushed unsalted roasted peanuts

❶ In a blender or food processor, combine the garlic, green onions, and ginger. Process until well minced. Add the tofu, peanut butter, soy sauce, vinegar, oil, ketchup, sugar, crushed red pepper, if using, and soy milk. Blend until smooth. Set aside.

❷ In a large pot of boiling salted water, cook the penne over medium-high heat, stirring occasionally, until al dente, about 10 minutes. About halfway through, add the carrots and broccoli to the boiling pasta. Drain the pasta and vegetables well and return to the pot.

❸ Pour the sauce over the pasta and vegetables. Toss to combine and cook over medium heat, stirring occasionally to heat through, about 5 minutes. Taste and adjust seasonings, if necessary. Sprinkle with the parsley and peanuts and serve.

Quick Lo Mein

<$2.00 per serving

Makes 4 servings

By using leftover cooked spaghetti or that ultimate cheap food, the ramen noodle brick, you can get this meal on the table in fifteen minutes or less. For an even quicker meal (and a great way to use bits of leftover veggies), toss in any cooked vegetables you may have on hand, such as steamed broccoli or green beans, in place of the cabbage.

4 cups cooked spaghetti or 3 (2.5-ounce) bricks ramen noodles	2 teaspoons grated fresh ginger
	1 medium carrot, shredded
16 ounces extra-firm tofu, drained and pressed	4 to 5 green onions, chopped
	4 cups shredded green cabbage
1 tablespoon cornstarch	1½ cups sliced white mushrooms
Salt	3 tablespoons soy sauce
2 tablespoons canola or other neutral oil	1 tablespoon rice vinegar
	1 tablespoon ketchup
2 garlic cloves, minced	1 teaspoon toasted sesame oil

1 If using ramen noodles, break the bricks into pieces and place them in a heatproof bowl. (Discard the seasoning packets.) Cover the noodles with boiling water and set aside.

2 Cut the tofu into ½-inch dice. Toss with the cornstarch and ¼ teaspoon salt and set aside.

3 In a large skillet, heat 1 tablespoon of the canola oil over medium-high heat. Add the tofu and cook until golden brown all over, about 7 minutes. Remove from the skillet and set aside.

4 In the same skillet, heat the remaining 1 tablespoon canola oil over medium-high heat. Add the garlic, ginger, carrot, green onions, cabbage, and mushrooms. Season with salt to taste, and stir-fry to soften, 4 to 5 minutes. Stir in the soy sauce, rice vinegar, ketchup, and sesame oil. Add the reserved tofu.

5 Add the spaghetti to the skillet. (If using ramen noodles, drain first and add to the skillet.) Toss to combine, adding a tablespoon or two of water if the mixture is too dry. Taste and adjust the seasonings, if necessary. Serve hot.

Splurge a Little

Replace the green cabbage with bok choy or napa cabbage.

Dan Dan–Style Linguine

<$2.00 per serving

Makes 4 servings

This spicy recipe is inspired by the spicy Szechuan noodle dish—*dan dan*—traditionally made with ground pork and preserved vegetables. Because many types of Chinese noodles contain eggs, I use linguine instead. Both hot chili oil and crushed red pepper are used in this recipe, so if you don't like your food too spicy, you'll want to cut back on the amount of each that you use.

8 ounces tempeh

4 tablespoons soy sauce

2 tablespoons tahini (sesame paste)

2 tablespoons creamy peanut butter

2 tablespoons hot chili oil

2 tablespoons rice vinegar

1 tablespoon sugar

1 teaspoon crushed red pepper

2 tablespoons canola or other neutral oil

12 ounces linguine

¼ cup minced onion

3 garlic cloves, minced

3 cups finely sliced bok choy or other greens

1 cup water

2 teaspoons toasted sesame oil

⅓ cup chopped unsalted roasted peanuts

4 green onions, chopped

3 tablespoons chopped fresh cilantro

1 In a medium saucepan of simmering water, cook the tempeh over medium heat for 30 minutes. Drain and let cool slightly.

2 Mince the tempeh into pea-size pieces and combine with 2 tablespoons of the soy sauce in a small bowl and mix well. Set aside.

3 In a separate small bowl, combine the tahini, peanut butter, the remaining 2 tablespoons of soy sauce, chili oil, vinegar, sugar, and crushed red pepper. Set aside.

4 In a large skillet, heat 1 tablespoon of the canola oil over medium-high heat. Add the tempeh and stir-fry until lightly browned, about 5 minutes. Remove from the skillet and set aside.

5 In a large pot of boiling salted water, cook the linguine over medium-high heat, stirring occasionally, until al dente, 8 to 10 minutes.

6 While the linguine is cooking, reheat the skillet with the remaining 1 tablespoon of canola oil. Add the onion and garlic and stir-fry for 1 minute. Add the bok choy and stir-fry for 1 minute. Add the reserved sauce mixture, stir in the water, and simmer for 5 minutes. Add the reserved tempeh to the sauce and simmer over very low heat.

7 When the linguine is cooked, drain well and return to the pot. Add the sesame oil and toss to combine. Place the linguine in a large serving bowl. To serve, top the noodles with the tempeh mixture and sprinkle with the peanuts, green onions, and cilantro.

Skillet Sense

A good skillet can be the gateway to a world of delicious meals. With a skillet, you can make Asian stir-fries, French sautés, Indian pilafs, and Italian risottos. You can also braise, fry, simmer, and poach a myriad of ingredients—all in one simple pan. A deep twelve-inch high-quality stainless steel skillet can handle most of these jobs well. A ten-inch cast iron skillet is also great to cook with—one with a baked-on enamel finish, if it's within your budget. You will, of course, also need a stockpot and a small and large saucepan, but for now let's focus on skillet cooking.

Skillet meals made with a variety of beans, grains, and vegetables can be especially kind to the food budget and because many of them are quick to prepare, they also economize on time and energy and can be lifesavers on busy nights.

In this chapter you will find homestyle favorites such as Skillet Hash (page 129), Stovetop Cheezee Mac (page 130), and Savory Sausage and Peppers (page 141), as well as more exotic fare such as Coconut Curry Rice (page 134), Tropic of Tempeh (page 147), and Penny-Pinching Pinto Picadillo (page 140), that are as delicious as they are easy on the wallet.

Perhaps the easiest skillet suppers are those made spontaneously with whatever is on hand. Sauté a little onion or garlic in oil, add chopped vegetables, tofu or seitan, and seasonings and serve over cooked grains or pasta. Within minutes, dinner can be on the table.

Sunday Supper Frittata

<$1.50 per serving

Makes 4 servings

You can make this versatile frittata with more, fewer, or different vegetables. I usually add whatever veggies are in the refrigerator. Cooked chopped broccoli or zucchini are good choices. While you can certainly make it without any vegetables at all, adding them makes this a more balanced meal. Serve topped with a drizzle of ketchup, if desired.

1 tablespoon olive oil
1 small yellow onion, minced
1 cup sliced white mushrooms
2 cups chopped fresh spinach
1 large potato, peeled, cooked, and chopped
Salt and black pepper
1 pound firm tofu, well drained

1 tablespoon plain unsweetened soy milk
2 tablespoons nutritional yeast
1 tablespoon cornstarch
½ teaspoon onion powder
½ teaspoon dried basil
½ teaspoon ground fennel seed (optional)
¼ teaspoon turmeric

1 Preheat the oven to 375°F. Lightly oil a 10-inch deep-dish pie plate or round 2-quart casserole dish and set aside.

2 In a large skillet, heat the oil over medium heat. Add the onion, cover, and cook until softened, about 10 minutes. Add the mushrooms and spinach and cook until the mushrooms are soft and the spinach is wilted, about 3 minutes.

3 Add the potato and cook to heat through, about 3 minutes longer. Season with salt and pepper to taste.

4 Spread the cooked vegetables into the bottom of the prepared baking dish and set aside.

5 In a blender, combine the tofu, soy milk, yeast, cornstarch, onion powder, basil, fennel, if using, and turmeric. Add ½ teaspoon of salt and ¼ teaspoon of pepper and blend until smooth.

6 Spread the tofu mixture evenly over the vegetables. Cover tightly with foil and bake for 30 minutes. Remove foil and bake 10 minutes longer to allow the top to become golden brown. Cut into wedges and serve hot.

Skillet Hash

<$1.00 per serving

Makes 4 servings

Hash makes an especially yummy brunch entrée, but it's delicious for lunch or dinner, as well. When I have leftover Slow-Cooker Seitan Pot Roast (page 213) and potatoes, this hash is usually on the menu the next day. If you have leftover cooked onion and carrots from the pot roast, you can substitute them for the raw ones in the recipe. Any kind of cooked potatoes can be used in this hash, such as russets, Yukon Golds, or sweet potatoes.

2 tablespoons olive oil

1 medium yellow onion, minced

2 medium carrots, grated

2 large or 3 medium potatoes, peeled, cooked, and chopped

2 cups cooked seitan (page 50), chopped

½ teaspoon dried marjoram

½ teaspoon ground fennel seed

½ teaspoon salt

¼ teaspoon black pepper

Ketchup, for serving

❶ In a large skillet, heat the oil over medium heat. Add the onion, cover, and cook until slightly softened, about 5 minutes. Add the carrots, cover, and cook until softened, about 5 minutes more.

❷ Add the potatoes, seitan, marjoram, fennel, salt, and pepper. Cook, uncovered, turning occasionally, until nicely browned, about 10 minutes. Taste and adjust seasonings, if necessary. Serve hot, drizzled with ketchup.

Splurge a Little

Sprinkle with shredded vegan mozzarella.

Stovetop Cheezee Mac

Makes 6 servings

This easy vegan mac and cheese is made on top of the stove and is ready to serve in minutes. If you prefer the crumb-topped baked version, use the variation below. Note: If your box of elbow macaroni contains 16 ounces, go ahead and cook the whole thing—you'll probably have enough sauce to coat it all, and the leftovers are great.

12 ounces elbow macaroni

1 cup firm tofu, drained

2½ cups plain unsweetened soy milk

½ cup nutritional yeast

2 tablespoons cornstarch

1 tablespoon fresh lemon juice

1 tablespoon apple cider vinegar

1 teaspoon yellow mustard

1 teaspoon salt

1 teaspoon onion powder

½ teaspoon garlic powder

½ teaspoon paprika

¼ teaspoon turmeric

¼ teaspoon ground cayenne

Black pepper

1 cup thawed frozen peas or 2 cups cooked chopped broccoli

1 (14.5-ounce) can diced tomatoes, drained (optional)

1 In a large pot of boiling salted water, cook the macaroni over medium-high heat, stirring occasionally, until al dente, about 8 minutes.

2 Meanwhile, in a blender, combine the tofu, soy milk, yeast, cornstarch, lemon juice, vinegar, mustard, salt, onion powder, garlic powder, paprika, turmeric, cayenne, and pepper to taste. Blend until smooth.

3 Drain the cooked macaroni and return it to the pot. Add the tofu mixture and peas and cook over medium heat, stirring, until the sauce comes to a boil and begins to thicken, about 4 minutes. Add a little more soy milk if too thick. Stir in the tomatoes, if using. Taste and adjust the seasonings, adding more salt if necessary. Simmer until hot. Serve immediately.

Variation

Oven-Baked Version: For a baked mac and cheese, transfer the mixture to a large baking dish, then top with about ½ cup bread crumbs and bake in a 375°F oven until the mixture is hot and the crumbs are browned.

Skillet Chili Mac

<$1.50 per serving

Makes 4 servings

Here's a great way to stretch leftovers from two of the recipes in this book. A small amount of chili and mac and cheese left from other meals join forces to make a third meal: a yummy chili mac that can be on the table in fifteen minutes.

2 cups prepared chili (see Note)
1½ cups cooked or 1 (15-ounce) can
    dark red kidney beans, drained
    and rinsed
1 cup tomato salsa, homemade
    (page 34) or store-bought

3 cups Stovetop Cheezee Mac
    (page 130)
2 tablespoons minced green onions
2 tablespoons chopped fresh
    cilantro

1 Combine the chili, beans, and salsa in a large deep skillet and cook over medium heat, stirring occasionally, until hot, about 7 minutes.

2 Stir in the mac and cheese and cook, stirring occasionally, until heated through, about 5 minutes. Serve hot sprinkled with green onions and cilantro.

Note: Use whatever chili you have on hand in the refrigerator or freezer, such as Black and White Bean Chili (page 78) or Positively Pantry Chili (page 205).

Splurge a Little
Garnish with a diced ripe avocado.

Salsa Rice and Red Beans

<$1.50 per serving

Makes 4 servings

This easy and flavorful skillet supper is ideal for busy weeknights. If you have rice that is already cooked, it can be put together even faster (just eliminate the 2 cups of water used for cooking the rice). For a real shortcut, use bottled tomato salsa in place of the onion, garlic, canned tomatoes, and chiles. If you can find tomato salsa on sale, this shortcut can save you money as well as time. Depending on the heat of your salsa and chiles, this can be as mild or as spicy as you like.

1 tablespoon olive oil

1 medium yellow onion, chopped

3 garlic cloves, chopped

1 cup long-grain brown rice

2 cups water

Salt

3 cups cooked or 2 (15.5-ounce) cans dark red kidney beans, drained and rinsed

1 (28-ounce) can diced tomatoes, drained

1 (4-ounce) can diced mild or hot green chiles, drained

1 teaspoon chili powder

½ teaspoon dried oregano

½ teaspoon ground cumin

¼ teaspoon black pepper

½ cup Cheezee Sauce (page 36; optional)

1 large ripe tomato, diced

3 green onions, minced (optional)

1 In a large skillet, heat the oil over medium heat. Add the onion, cover, and cook until softened, about 5 minutes. Add the garlic and cook for 30 seconds longer. Stir in the rice and water. Add salt to taste, cover, and simmer until the rice is tender, 35 to 45 minutes.

2 Stir in the beans, tomatoes, chiles, chili powder, oregano, cumin, and pepper. Simmer to heat through and blend the flavors, about 10 minutes. Taste and adjust the seasonings, if necessary.

3 Serve hot, drizzled with the cheezee sauce, if using, the diced tomato, and the green onions, if using.

Splurge a Little

Garnish with a diced ripe avocado.

Curried Red Bean Pilaf with Walnuts and Raisins

<$1.00 per serving

Makes 4 servings

Rice and beans is one of the most economical and nutritious meals on the planet, and there are lots of ways to add variety to this dynamic duo. This recipe, seasoned with curry powder, raisins, and walnuts, is one delicious way, but don't stop there. Variations can include omitting the curry in favor of other spice blends or herbs, using a different type of bean, and adding different vegetables.

1 tablespoon olive oil
1 small yellow onion, minced
2 green onions, minced
1 cup long-grain brown rice
2 to 3 teaspoons hot or mild curry powder
2 cups vegetable stock (page 45)
1½ cups cooked or 1 (15.5-ounce) can dark red kidney beans, drained and rinsed

1 cup thawed frozen green peas
⅓ cup golden raisins
⅓ cup toasted walnut pieces
Salt and black pepper

❶ In a medium saucepan, heat the oil over medium heat. Add the onion, cover, and cook until softened, about 5 minutes. Add the green onions and cook for 1 minute. Add the rice and curry powder, stirring to coat. Stir in the stock and bring to a boil.

❷ Cover, reduce heat to low, and simmer until the rice is tender and the liquid is absorbed, 35 to 45 minutes.

❸ Remove from the heat. Stir in the beans, peas, raisins, and walnuts. Season with salt and pepper to taste. Serve hot.

Coconut Curry Rice

<$1.50 per serving

Makes 4 servings

The richness of coconut milk can go a long way to making a simple meal of rice and chickpeas seem like a restaurant meal. If you're not a fan of curry, leave out the curry powder and the tomatoes for a luscious coconut-centric rice dish.

1 tablespoon olive oil	Salt
½ cup minced onion	1½ cups cooked or 1 (15-ounce) can
1 garlic clove, minced	chickpeas, drained and rinsed
2 to 3 teaspoons hot or mild curry	1 (14.5-ounce) can diced tomatoes,
powder	drained
1 cup long-grain brown rice	½ cup thawed frozen peas
½ cup vegetable stock (page 45)	Black pepper
1 (13-ounce) can unsweetened	⅓ cup unsalted roasted cashews
coconut milk	

1 In a medium saucepan, heat the oil over medium heat. Add the onion, cover, and cook until softened, about 5 minutes. Stir in the garlic and curry powder and cook for 30 seconds.

2 Stir in the rice, then add the stock and coconut milk and bring just to a boil over medium-high heat. Reduce heat to medium and season with salt to taste. Cover and simmer until the rice is tender, 35 to 45 minutes.

3 Stir in the chickpeas, tomatoes, and peas. Season with salt and pepper to taste, and add more curry powder, if necessary. Cook, uncovered, to allow flavors to blend, about 10 minutes. Serve hot, sprinkled with cashews.

White Bean and Barley "Risotto" with Kale and Tempeh

<$1.50 per serving

Makes 4 to 6 servings

Traditional risotto uses Arborio rice, which is expensive. When you use barley instead, you save money and get to enjoy a nutritious grain in a deliciously different way. Including kale, beans, and tempeh makes this a hearty one-dish meal.

2 tablespoons olive oil
1 cup finely chopped onion
1 garlic clove, minced
8 ounces white mushrooms, sliced
1 cup pearl barley
4 cups vegetable stock (page 45)
Salt
3 cups finely chopped kale

1½ cups or 1 (15.5-ounce) can white beans, drained and rinsed
1 cup Smoky Tempeh Bits (page 58)
¼ cup plain unsweetened soy milk
1 tablespoon vegan margarine
1½ teaspoons dried savory
Black pepper

1 In a large skillet, heat the oil over medium heat. Add the onion, cover, and cook until tender, about 5 minutes. Add the garlic and mushrooms and cook until tender, about 3 minutes.

2 Stir in the barley and 3 cups of the stock. Season with salt to taste (the amount of salt needed depends on the saltiness of your stock). Bring to a boil over high heat, then reduce the heat to low, cover, and cook, stirring occasionally, until the barley is tender and most of the stock is absorbed, about 45 minutes. About halfway through the cooking time, stir in the kale. If the stock is absorbed before the barley is tender, add as much of the remaining cup of stock as needed and cook until the barley is soft. Stir in the beans and tempeh bits and simmer until heated through, about 3 minutes.

3 When the barley is tender, remove from the heat and stir in the soy milk, margarine, and savory. Season with salt and pepper to taste, and serve at once.

Splurge a Little

Use fresh porcini mushrooms instead of white. Add 1 cup chopped cooked artichoke hearts when you add the tempeh.

Moroccan Chickpeas and Couscous

Makes 4 servings

When you keep your pantry stocked with quick-cooking couscous, canned tomatoes, and chickpeas, an easy and inexpensive dinner is always less than fifteen minutes away. Variations include adding a sliced or shredded carrot when you cook the onion, or adding a cup or two of cooked vegetables such as green beans, spinach, or broccoli when you add the chickpeas. The old standby, frozen peas, makes a colorful and tasty add-in as well.

1½ cups water
Salt
1 (10-ounce) box couscous
1 tablespoon olive oil
1 large onion, chopped
5 green onions, chopped
2 garlic cloves, minced
2 tablespoons minced jalapeño or other hot chile (optional)
1 teaspoon grated fresh ginger
1 (14-ounce) can diced tomatoes, drained

1½ cups cooked or 1 (15.5-ounce) can chickpeas, drained and rinsed
½ cup golden raisins
1 teaspoon sugar
¾ teaspoon ground cumin
¾ teaspoon ground coriander
¼ teaspoon black pepper
¼ cup chopped fresh parsley or cilantro
2 tablespoons toasted sliced almonds

❶ In a medium saucepan, bring the water to boil over high heat. Stir in salt to taste and the couscous, cover, and remove from the heat.

❷ In a large skillet, heat the oil over medium heat. Add the onion, cover, and cook until softened, about 5 minutes. Add the green onions, garlic, jalapeño, if using, and ginger. Cook, stirring until softened, about 3 minutes.

❸ Add the tomatoes, chickpeas, raisins, sugar, cumin, coriander, ¼ teaspoon salt, and pepper. Cook, stirring to heat through and blend the flavors, about 10 minutes.

❹ To serve, spoon the cooked couscous into a shallow serving bowl or individual bowls, spoon the chickpea mixture on top, and sprinkle with the parsley and almonds.

Simple Skillet Suppers

Whenever you have a small amount of leftovers, such as cooked vegetables, rice, pasta, or a leftover baked potato, think skillet supper. Just take the ingredients in question, and build from there. Start by sautéing some chopped onion or garlic in oil. If you've got rice, you can make a simple fried rice dish by adding some grated carrot, frozen peas, and crumbled tofu; a little ginger if you have it; Asian chili paste if you like heat. Season with soy sauce and a little sesame oil. Change up the seasonings according to what you're in the mood for (maybe some curry?) or let the ingredients help dictate the dish—nothing says "hash" like leftover baked potatoes and seitan. For leftover pasta, add a can of diced tomatoes to your sautéing onion and garlic along with some basil and oregano. Add some cooked white beans or crumbled vegan sausage and a few chopped pitted olives to simmer with the pasta.

Polenta with Pan-Seared Mushrooms and Tomatoes

<$1.50 per serving

Makes 4 servings

Polenta is the quintessential peasant food of Italy. It is delicious, filling, and economical. When I was a child, my mother served it "family style"—spread on a large bread board the size of the kitchen table and topped with tomato sauce. The whole family sat around the table and ate from the communal board. This recipe is served in a less rustic manner, but is no less delicious.

3½ cups water

1 cup medium-ground yellow cornmeal

Salt

¼ cup plain unsweetened soy milk

2 tablespoons vegan margarine

2 tablespoons olive oil

8 ounces white mushrooms, sliced

2 garlic cloves, minced

1 teaspoon dried savory

1 teaspoon dried basil

Black pepper

¼ cup dry white wine

1 (28-ounce) can Italian-style diced tomatoes, drained

1 In a large saucepan, bring the water to boil over high heat. Reduce heat to a simmer and add the cornmeal and salt to taste, stirring constantly. Cook, stirring, until thick, about 20 minutes. During the last 5 minutes of cooking, stir in the soy milk and margarine. Keep warm.

2 While the polenta is cooking, heat 1 tablespoon of the oil in a large skillet over medium-high heat. Add the mushrooms and sear on both sides. Reduce the heat to medium, and add the garlic, savory, basil, and salt and pepper to taste. Stir in the wine, then add the tomatoes and simmer to heat through and blend the flavors, about 10 minutes. Taste and adjust the seasonings, if necessary, and keep warm.

3 To serve, spoon the polenta into shallow bowls and top with the mushroom-tomato mixture. Serve hot.

Note: Cornmeal for polenta comes in different grinds. They all require slightly different amounts of water and cooking times. If you have something other than medium-ground polenta cornmeal, simply follow your package directions.

Indian-Spiced Lentil Ragu

<$2.00 per serving

Makes 4 servings

Multiple flavor layers transform everyday lentils into a special dish that is especially good served over fragrant basmati rice to catch every drop of the delicious sauce.

¾ cup brown lentils

1 (10-ounce) package frozen spinach, thawed

2 tablespoons canola or other neutral oil

1 medium yellow onion, chopped

2 garlic cloves, minced

1½ teaspoons grated fresh ginger

1 tablespoon hot or mild curry powder

½ teaspoon ground coriander

¼ teaspoon ground cumin

1 (14.5-ounce) can diced tomatoes, undrained

½ teaspoon salt

¼ teaspoon black pepper

½ cup plain vegan yogurt

1 Bring a medium saucepan of salted water to boil over high heat. Add the lentils, return to a boil, then reduce heat to low. Cover and cook until tender, 40 to 45 minutes. During the last 5 minutes of cooking, add the spinach. Drain and set aside.

2 In a large skillet, heat the oil over medium heat. Add the onion, cover, and cook until tender, about 7 minutes.

3 Stir in the garlic, ginger, curry powder, coriander, and cumin. Cook for 1 minute, then add the tomatoes with their juice and cook, stirring to blend the flavors, for 5 minutes. Stir in the cooked lentils and spinach, salt, and pepper. Simmer until the mixture is hot and the flavors are blended, about 10 minutes. Taste and adjust the seasoning, adding a bit more curry powder or salt if necessary. Serve hot with the yogurt on the side.

Splurge a Little

Use fresh spinach instead of frozen, adding it when you add the tomatoes.

Penny-Pinching Pinto Picadillo

Makes 4 servings

Picadillo is popular in many Central and South American countries as well as the Philippines, with each region having its own variation. Traditionally made with ground beef, its name comes from the Spanish *picar,* meaning "to chop." My version uses pinto beans to replace the ground beef and adds rice to the dish instead of serving it on the side. This is a great way to use leftover baked or roasted potatoes and cooked rice. (If using cooked rice or potatoes, just skip over the cooking instructions for those ingredients.)

2 cups water

1 cup long-grain brown rice

Salt

2 russet potatoes, diced

2 tablespoons olive oil

1 medium yellow onion, chopped

3 garlic cloves, minced

1½ cups cooked or 1 (15.5-ounce) can pinto beans, drained and rinsed

1 (28-ounce) can diced tomatoes with chiles, drained

⅓ cup pimento-stuffed green olives, sliced

⅓ cup raisins

1 teaspoon ground cumin

¼ teaspoon ground cinnamon

¼ teaspoon black pepper

1 In a large saucepan, bring the water to boil over high heat. Add the rice and salt to taste. Reduce the heat to medium-low, cover, and simmer until tender, about 35 minutes. Set aside.

2 Steam the potatoes until tender, about 10 minutes. Set aside.

3 In a large skillet, heat the oil over medium heat. Add the onion, cover, and cook until soft, about 7 minutes. Add the garlic and potatoes and cook, uncovered, for 5 minutes. Add the beans, tomatoes, olives, and raisins. Stir in the cumin, cinnamon, ½ teaspoon salt, and pepper, mixing well to combine.

4 Add the cooked rice and cook, stirring, until the mixture is hot. Taste and adjust seasonings. Serve hot.

Variations

Substitute finely chopped sautéed seitan for the pinto beans. Omit the rice from the recipe and instead, serve the rice alongside the picadillo. The picadillo mixture can also be used as a filling for tacos.

Savory Sausage and Peppers

<$1.50 per serving

Makes 4 servings

This recipe can be enjoyed in a number of ways: Cut the vegetables and sausage smaller to use as a sauce for pasta, or leave the pieces larger to enjoy as a stew over rice or another grain. For a less saucy version, leave out the vegetable stock. Tempeh or seitan can be used instead of the sausage, if you prefer.

2 tablespoons olive oil

3 Close to Mom's Sausage links (variation; page 54), diced

1 medium yellow onion, chopped

1 medium carrot, thinly sliced

2 medium green bell peppers, diced

1 medium russet potato, thinly sliced

3 garlic cloves, minced

½ teaspoon dried thyme

½ teaspoon dried marjoram

½ teaspoon salt

¼ teaspoon black pepper

1 (14.5-ounce) can diced tomatoes, undrained

½ cup vegetable stock (page 45)

2 tablespoons soy sauce

❶ In a large skillet, heat 1 tablespoon of the oil over medium heat. Add sausage and cook until browned. Remove from the skillet and set aside.

❷ Heat the remaining oil in the same skillet over medium heat. Add the onion and carrot, cover, and cook until softened, 5 minutes. Add the bell peppers, potato, garlic, thyme, marjoram, salt, and black pepper. Cover and cook until softened, about 10 minutes.

❸ Stir in the tomatoes with their juice and stock and simmer, uncovered, until the vegetables are tender, about 8 minutes. Stir in the cooked sausage. Taste and adjust the seasonings, if necessary. Cook until heated through. Serve hot.

Splurge a Little

Substitute packaged vegan sausage (such as Tofurky brand) for the homemade sausage links.

Better-Than-Takeout Tofu Stir-Fry

<$1.50 per serving

Makes 4 servings

When you crave a tasty stir-fry, save the money on takeout, and make this recipe instead. If you have leftover veggies, you can use them instead of the broccoli and carrots.

3 cups small broccoli florets

1 large carrot, thinly sliced

1 pound extra-firm tofu, drained and pressed

⅓ cup plus 1 tablespoon cornstarch

Canola oil, for frying

4 green onions, chopped

2 garlic cloves, minced

¾ teaspoon grated fresh ginger

1 cup vegetable stock (page 45)

¼ cup soy sauce

1½ to 2 tablespoons light brown sugar

2 tablespoons rice vinegar

2 tablespoons dry sherry

1 tablespoon ketchup

1 teaspoon toasted sesame oil

½ teaspoon Asian chili paste (optional)

2 tablespoons water

Freshly cooked rice

1 Steam the broccoli and carrot until just tender, about 5 minutes. Run under cold water to stop the cooking process and set aside.

2 Cut the tofu into 1-inch dice and place in a medium bowl. Sprinkle the ⅓ cup cornstarch over the tofu and toss gently to coat.

3 In a large skillet, heat a thin layer of the canola oil over medium heat. Add the tofu and cook until golden brown, about 8 minutes. Remove the tofu from the skillet with a slotted spoon and set aside.

4 Heat 1 tablespoon of canola oil in the same skillet over medium heat. Add the green onions, garlic, and ginger, and cook until softened, about 2 minutes. Stir in the stock, soy sauce, sugar, vinegar, sherry, ketchup, sesame oil, and chili paste, if using. Combine the remaining 1 tablespoon cornstarch with the 2 tablespoons water and pour into the sauce, stirring to thicken. Add the cooked tofu along with the steamed broccoli and carrot. Stir-fry to heat through and coat evenly with the sauce, about 4 minutes. Serve hot over rice.

Tofu Fried Rice

<$1.50 per serving

Makes 4 servings

Cold cooked rice is a must for good fried rice and a great reason to prepare extra any time you're making rice. Chopped leftover cooked vegetables (especially broccoli) make a good addition.

¼ cup soy sauce
2 tablespoons ketchup
2 tablespoons rice vinegar
2 teaspoons toasted sesame oil
1 tablespoon canola or other
    neutral oil
1 medium yellow onion, finely
    chopped
2 medium carrots, thinly sliced
4 garlic cloves, minced

4 ounces white mushrooms,
    chopped
1 teaspoon grated fresh ginger
8 ounces extra-firm tofu, drained
    and crumbled
3 cups cold cooked rice
1 cup thawed frozen peas
Salt and black pepper

❶ In a small bowl, combine the soy sauce, ketchup, vinegar, and sesame oil and set aside.

❷ In a large skillet, heat the canola oil over medium heat. Add the onion and carrots, cover, and cook until softened, about 5 minutes. Uncover, and stir in the garlic, mushrooms, and ginger. Add the tofu and cook, stirring, for 4 to 5 minutes. Add the soy sauce mixture, stirring to coat.

❸ Add the rice and peas. Stir-fry until well mixed and heated through. Season with salt and pepper, and taste and adjust the seasoning, adding more soy sauce if necessary. Serve immediately.

Walnut-Crusted Tofu with Spinach and Orange

<$2.00 per serving

Makes 4 servings

A crunchy and flavorful walnut crust transforms tofu into a sophisticated dinner entrée. Either seitan or tempeh can be used to replace the tofu in this recipe. Serve with basmati rice, quinoa, or roasted potatoes. Note: I like to use fresh spinach in this recipe, but you can substitute the more economical frozen spinach (cooked according to package directions) if you prefer.

1 pound extra-firm tofu, drained and cut into ½-inch slices
Salt and black pepper
⅔ cup dry bread crumbs
⅓ cup ground walnuts
2 tablespoons soy sauce
1½ tablespoons Dijon mustard
1½ tablespoons pure maple syrup

1 tablespoon Make-Your-Own Mayo (page 41)
⅓ cup all-purpose flour
3 tablespoons olive oil
9 ounces fresh spinach, trimmed
2 navel oranges, peeled and sectioned (see page 87)
½ teaspoon ground sage or 6 fresh sage leaves, chopped

❶ Press any remaining liquid from the tofu slices and blot them dry. Season with salt and pepper to taste, and set aside. Preheat the oven to 250°F.

❷ In a shallow bowl, combine the bread crumbs and walnuts and mix well. In a shallow bowl, combine the soy sauce, mustard, maple syrup, and mayonnaise, stirring to blend well. Place the flour in a separate shallow bowl.

❸ One at a time, dip the tofu slices into the flour, shaking off any excess. Then dip the tofu slices in the mustard mixture, coating all over, then place them in the walnut mixture, turning to coat, lightly pressing the walnut mixture into the tofu.

❹ In a large skillet, heat 2 tablespoons of the oil over medium-high heat. Add the tofu slices and cook until golden brown on both sides, turning once, about 4 minutes per side. Transfer to a baking sheet and keep warm in the oven. Repeat with all the tofu.

5 Heat the remaining oil in the same skillet over medium heat. Add the spinach and toss until wilted. Stir in the orange sections, sage, and salt and pepper to taste. To serve, top the tofu with the spinach and orange mixture. Serve hot.

Splurge a Little

Add 2 tablespoons of capers when you add the orange sections. Use panko instead of regular bread crumbs. For convenience, use bottled vegan mayonnaise instead of homemade.

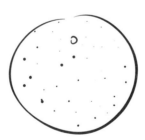

Barbecued Black Bean and Tofu Burritos

Makes 4 servings

This easy and inexpensive dinner has the smoky-sweet barbecue flavor the kids will love all wrapped up in soft flour tortillas. Thin strips of crisp-fried extra-firm tofu add texture and nutrition. Serve with a bowl of slaw and some tortilla chips for a quick weeknight meal. Liquid smoke is a seasoning liquid available in supermarkets that adds a smoky flavor to foods.

2 tablespoons olive oil

1 small yellow onion, chopped

2 tablespoons ketchup

1 tablespoon molasses

1 tablespoon Dijon mustard

2 tablespoons soy sauce

1 teaspoon light brown sugar

½ teaspoon liquid smoke

Salt and black pepper

1½ cups cooked or 1 (15.5-ounce) can black beans, drained and rinsed

8 ounces extra-firm tofu, drained and pressed

4 (10-inch) flour tortillas

❶ In a large saucepan, heat 1 tablespoon of the oil over medium heat. Add the onion, cover, and cook until soft. Stir in the ketchup, molasses, mustard, 1 tablespoon of the soy sauce, sugar, liquid smoke, and salt and pepper to taste. Add the beans and cook, stirring occasionally, until hot and well mixed. Taste and adjust seasonings, if necessary. Set aside and keep warm.

❷ Cut the tofu into ¼-inch strips. Heat the remaining oil in a large skillet over medium-high heat. Add the tofu and cook until golden brown, turning as needed. Season with salt and pepper to taste, and sprinkle with the remaining 1 tablespoon of soy sauce.

❸ To serve, divide the tofu strips among the tortillas and spoon the bean mixture on top of the tofu. Roll up the tortillas and serve hot.

Tropic of Tempeh

<$2.00 per serving

Makes 4 servings

The pineapple and fragrant spices in the sauce add a taste of the trop-
ics to this easy and economical tempeh preparation that tastes great
served over rice or other cooked grain.

8 ounces tempeh

⅓ cup cornstarch

1 (16-ounce) can pineapple chunks,
    liquid reserved

3 tablespoons rice vinegar

2 tablespoons soy sauce

1 tablespoon light brown sugar

½ teaspoon thyme

½ teaspoon allspice

¼ teaspoon ground cayenne

3 tablespoons canola or other
    neutral oil

2 large carrots, sliced

1 large yellow onion, sliced

1 large green bell pepper, diced

3 garlic cloves, minced

½ cup chopped green onions

2 teaspoons grated fresh ginger

1 In a medium saucepan of simmering water, cook the tempeh over medium
heat for 30 minutes. Drain, pat dry, and set aside. When cool enough
to handle, cut the tempeh into 1-inch dice and place in a shallow bowl.
Sprinkle with the cornstarch and toss to coat.

2 In a food processor, combine half of the pineapple chunks (reserve the
liquid) with the rice vinegar, soy sauce, sugar, thyme, allspice, and cayenne. Process until smooth. Set aside.

3 In a large skillet, heat 2 tablespoons of the oil over medium heat. Add the
tempeh and stir-fry until golden brown, about 5 minutes. Remove from the
skillet and set aside.

4 Add the remaining oil to the same skillet over medium heat. Add the carrots, onion, and bell pepper, and stir-fry until softened, about 5 minutes.
Add the garlic, green onions, and ginger and stir-fry for 30 seconds
more.

5 Pour in the reserved pineapple juice and stir-fry until the liquid is reduced
by half, about 5 minutes. Add the cooked tempeh, the remaining pineapple, and the reserved sauce and toss to coat and heat through. Serve
immediately.

Mu Shu Burritos

<$1.50 per serving

Makes 4 servings

Flour tortillas replace delicate mu shu pancakes in a non-traditional interpretation of the classic Chinese dish flavored with fragrant sweet hoisin sauce. The delicious seitan and cabbage filling can be enjoyed over rice instead of rolled in the tortillas, if you prefer.

2 tablespoons canola or other neutral oil

8 ounces shredded seitan (page 50)

1 small head green cabbage, finely shredded (about 4 cups)

1 large carrot, shredded

4 green onions, chopped

¼ cup hoisin sauce, plus more for serving

¼ cup water

1 tablespoon toasted sesame oil

8 (7-inch) flour tortillas

1. In a large skillet or wok, heat 1 tablespoon of the canola oil over medium heat. Add the seitan and cook until browned. Remove from the skillet and set aside.

2. Heat the remaining 1 tablespoon canola oil in the same skillet. Add the cabbage, carrot, and green onions and cook until softened, about 7 minutes.

3. In a small bowl, combine the hoisin sauce, water, and sesame oil, stirring to blend. Pour the hoisin mixture into the skillet. Add the reserved seitan and stir-fry to coat, about 3 minutes. Cook a few minutes longer until the flavors are blended.

4. To serve, spread a thin line of hoisin sauce down the center of each tortilla. Arrange about ½ cup of the seitan and cabbage mixture along the center of each tortilla. Tuck in the sides and roll up like a burrito. Serve at once.

Splurge a Little

Use napa cabbage instead of green cabbage.

Smoky Tempeh with Cabbage and Potatoes

Makes 4 servings

This stick-to-your-ribs skillet supper is terrific for cold winter nights. I like to serve it with a bowl of warm homemade applesauce fragrant with cinnamon.

1 tablespoon olive oil	⅓ cup water
1 medium yellow onion, chopped	Salt and black pepper
1 small head green cabbage, shredded	1 recipe Smoky Tempeh Bits (page 58)
3 Yukon Gold potatoes, diced	

1 In a large skillet, heat oil over medium heat. Add the onion, cover, and cook until softened, about 5 minutes. Add the cabbage, potatoes, water, and salt and pepper to taste. Cover and cook until softened, about 12 minutes.

2 Uncover and continue cooking until the vegetables are soft, about 5 minutes. Add the tempeh bits. Taste and adjust the seasonings, if necessary, and cook until flavors are blended, about 10 minutes longer. Serve immediately.

Variation

Substitute sauteed sliced vegan sausage links for the Smoky Tempeh Bits.

Splurge a Little

Use Savoy cabbage instead of green cabbage.

First-Class Bakes and Casseroles

*T*o many of us, a casserole is the ultimate comfort food, warming the house while it bakes and filling the air with its tantalizing aroma. But oven-baked meals have additional virtues as well. They tend to be versatile, easy to make, and economical. Best of all, most can be assembled ahead of time, which cuts down on messy cleanup after dinner.

For all these reasons, these are among my favorite go-to recipes when I need to feed a crowd. For casual weeknight dinners, there's Baked Ziti (page 160) and Mexican Rice and Bean Bake (page 159). When you're having guests for dinner, the casserole can go first class, with Torta Rustica (page 172) and Deluxe Vegetable Lasagna (page 162) among the tasty offerings. For something different and delicious try the ultimate stuffed mushrooms, Essence of Porcini–Stuffed Dinner Mushrooms (page 157) or the sassy Smoky Southwest Sweet Potato Shepherd's Pie (page 153). And don't forget the Comfort Loaf (page 154), a vegan version of a homey meatloaf—it's great with the Creamy Mushroom Gravy (page 31). Saving money on your food bill never tasted so good.

Baked Potato Bar

The baked potato bar is perhaps one of the best budget-stretching meal ideas ever conceived. To do one at home, simply scrub some rus-set potatoes, pat them dry, prick with a fork, and rub with a little oil, if desired (this is optional). Bake in a 400°F oven until tender, 45 minutes to an hour. While the potatoes are baking, assemble a variety of top-pings. Be creative. Look through the freezer, refrigerator, and cupboard to come up with topping ideas:

heated leftover chili or stew

vegan sour cream and chives

vegan yogurt blended with a little curry powder and chutney

Cheezee Sauce (page 36) tossed with cooked chopped broccoli

caramelized onions

pesto

Easy Peanut Sauce (page 40)

salsa

Once the potatoes are done, everyone can enjoy them "their way"—and you can chalk up another delicious and inexpensive meal. If any potatoes are left over, slice them and fry them up for dinner the next night, maybe with some lemon juice and oregano.

Smoky Southwest Sweet Potato Shepherd's Pie

<$1.50 per serving

Makes 4 to 6 servings

Shepherd's pie takes a decidedly unconventional turn with a spicy chipotle sweet–potato topping and a black bean filling with Southwest flavors.

3 sweet potatoes, peeled and cut into ½-inch dice

2 chipotle chiles in adobo

2 tablespoons water

2 tablespoons vegan margarine

Salt and black pepper

1 tablespoon olive oil

1 medium yellow onion, finely chopped

2 medium carrots, chopped

3 cups cooked or 2 (15.5-ounce) cans black beans, drained and rinsed

1½ cups thawed frozen corn kernels

1½ cups tomato salsa

½ teaspoon ground cumin

1 Preheat the oven to 350°F. Lightly oil a 9 × 13-inch baking pan and set aside. Steam the potatoes until just tender, about 12 minutes. While the potatoes are steaming, in a blender or food processor, puree the chiles with the water and set aside.

2 Mash the steamed potatoes with half of the chipotle puree, the margarine, and salt and pepper to taste. Set aside.

3 In a large skillet, heat the oil over medium heat. Add the onion and carrots, cover, and cook until soft, about 10 minutes. Transfer to the prepared pan. Add the beans, corn, salsa, cumin, and the remaining chipotle puree. Season with salt and pepper to taste. Stir to combine.

4 Spread the mashed potatoes evenly on top of the bean mixture. Bake until the filling is hot, about 40 minutes. Serve hot.

Comfort Loaf

<$1.00 per serving

Makes 6 servings

Meatloaf has long been synonymous with economical comfort food. This loaf skips the meat, of course, and is loaded with comfort. Serve with Creamy Mushroom Gravy (page 31) and accompany with mashed potatoes and a green vegetable such as broccoli or green beans. Leftovers make great sandwiches.

2 tablespoons olive oil

1 medium onion, minced

2 celery ribs, minced

1 medium carrot, minced

1 garlic clove, minced

1½ cups cooked or 1 (15.5-ounce) can pinto beans, drained, rinsed, and mashed

1 pound extra-firm tofu, drained and crumbled

2 tablespoons soy sauce

2 tablespoons tomato paste

1 tablespoon yellow or spicy brown mustard

½ cup ground walnuts

½ cup old-fashioned oats

½ cup dry bread crumbs

½ cup wheat gluten flour (vital wheat gluten)

¼ cup chopped fresh parsley

1 tablespoon dried basil

1 tablespoon dried thyme

1 tablespoon dried savory

1 teaspoon salt

½ teaspoon black pepper

❶ Preheat the oven to 375°F. Lightly oil a 9-inch loaf pan and set aside.

❷ In a large skillet, heat the oil over medium heat. Add the onion, celery, carrot, and garlic. Cover and cook until softened, about 10 minutes. Stir in the beans, mixing well to combine. Remove from the heat and set aside.

❸ In a food processor, combine the tofu, soy sauce, tomato paste, and mustard and process until smooth. Set aside.

❹ In a large bowl, combine the walnuts, oats, bread crumbs, and flour. Add the parsley, basil, thyme, savory, salt, and pepper. Stir in the tofu mixture and the vegetables and mix well to combine.

❺ Scrape the mixture evenly into the prepared pan and smooth the top. Bake until firm, 45 to 50 minutes. If the top begins to brown too much, cover loosely with foil. Remove from the oven and set aside for 10 minutes on a wire rack before slicing.

Three-Bean Loaf

<$1.00
per serving

Makes 6 servings

A tangy sweet topping graces this wholesome and economical loaf. As long as you have the oven turned on, make some roasted potatoes, carrots, and Brussels sprouts as accompaniments. Serve with Creamy Mushroom Gravy (page 31) or ketchup.

1 tablespoon olive oil
1 medium yellow onion, finely
   chopped
1 medium carrot, finely chopped
1 celery rib, finely chopped
4 garlic cloves, minced
1½ cups cooked or 1 (15.5-ounce)
   can chickpeas, drained and
   rinsed
1½ cups cooked or 1 (15.5-ounce)
   can black beans, drained and
   rinsed
1½ cups cooked or 1 (15.5-ounce)
   can dark red kidney beans,
   drained and rinsed

½ cup ketchup
2 tablespoons soy sauce
½ teaspoon salt
½ teaspoon black pepper
1 cup dry bread crumbs
½ cup old-fashioned oats
½ cup wheat gluten flour (vital
   wheat gluten)
½ cup chopped fresh parsley
2 tablespoons yellow or spicy
   brown mustard
1 tablespoon light brown sugar
2 teaspoons apple cider vinegar

❶ Preheat the oven to 375°F. Lightly oil a 9-inch loaf pan and set aside.

❷ In a large skillet, heat the oil over medium heat. Add the onion, carrot, celery, and garlic. Cover and cook until softened, about 10 minutes. Remove from heat and set aside.

❸ Place the three varieties of beans in a large bowl. Mash well, leaving some texture. Add the onion-carrot mixture, then stir in ¼ cup of the ketchup, soy sauce, salt, and pepper. Add the bread crumbs, oats, flour, and parsley and mix until well combined. Spread the mixture evenly in the prepared pan and smooth the top.

❹ In a small bowl, combine the remaining ¼ cup ketchup with the mustard, sugar, and vinegar and mix well. Spread the topping mixture on top of the loaf. Bake until firm, 50 to 60 minutes. If the top begins to brown too much, cover loosely with foil. Remove from the oven and set aside on a wire rack for 10 minutes before slicing.

Tortilla Strata

<$1.50 per serving

Makes 4 to 6 servings

Flour tortillas are ideal for layering, and layering is what a strata is all about. Use this recipe as a guide to add extra layers of other ingredients you may have on hand, such as cooked potatoes or spinach—almost anything tastes great layered with salsa and tortillas! I use a 10-inch springform pan for visual appeal, but you can simply layer the ingredients in a large round casserole dish, if you prefer.

1 (24-ounce) jar tomato salsa

5 (10-inch) flour tortillas

1½ cups cooked brown rice

1½ cups cooked or 1 (15.5-ounce) can dark red kidney beans, drained and rinsed

1½ cups fresh or thawed frozen corn kernels

1 (4-ounce) can mild minced green chiles, drained

⅔ cup Cheezee Sauce (page 36)

1 Preheat the oven to 350°F. Lightly oil a 10-inch springform pan or 2½-quart casserole dish.

2 Spoon about ⅔ cup of the salsa in the bottom of the prepared pan. Top with 1 tortilla and set aside.

3 In a large bowl, combine the rice with half the beans and ½ cup of the salsa. Stir to mix. Spread half of the rice mixture onto the tortilla in the pan and top with another tortilla. Spread about ⅔ cup of salsa on the top tortilla and set aside.

4 In a separate large bowl, combine the remaining beans with the corn and chiles. Add ⅓ cup of the cheezee sauce and stir to mix. Spread half of the corn mixture on top of the tortilla in the pan and top with another tortilla.

5 Repeat with remaining ingredients, ending with a layer of salsa on top. Drizzle with the remaining cheezee sauce. Cover with foil and bake until hot, about 45 minutes. Let sit for 10 minutes. If using a springform pan, carefully remove the sides. Serve hot.

Splurge a Little

Use shredded vegan cheddar cheese instead of the cheezee sauce. Garnish with diced avocado.

Essence of Porcini–Stuffed Dinner Mushrooms

<$1.50 per serving

Makes 4 servings

Enjoy the luxurious flavor of fresh porcini mushrooms without the expense by making powder from dried porcinis. To make about 2 tablespoons of porcini powder, place 1 dried porcini mushroom in a spice mill and grind to a powder.

¼ cup soy sauce

2 tablespoons olive oil

1 tablespoon plus 1 teaspoon dried porcini powder

4 large portobello mushrooms, lightly rinsed, patted dry (reserve and chop stems)

¼ cup chopped onion

1 garlic clove, minced

½ teaspoon dried thyme

Salt and black pepper

1 cup cooked or canned white beans, drained and rinsed

4 tablespoons dry bread crumbs

1 Preheat the oven to 425°F. Lightly oil a 9 × 13-inch baking pan.

2 Combine the soy sauce, 1 tablespoon of the oil, and 1 teaspoon of the porcini powder in the prepared pan. Dip the mushroom caps in the soy sauce mixture and arrange them in the dish, cut side up. Bake for 15 minutes.

3 While the mushrooms are baking, heat the remaining 1 tablespoon oil in a large skillet. Add onion, cover, and cook until softened, 5 minutes. Add the garlic, chopped mushroom stems, thyme, remaining porcini powder, and salt and pepper to taste. Cook, stirring, for 3 minutes.

4 In a medium bowl, mash the beans. Stir the mashed beans into the stuffing mixture. Mix well to combine.

5 Remove the mushroom caps from the oven and spoon the stuffing mixture into the caps. Top each mushroom with the bread crumbs, pressing on the crumbs so they adhere to the stuffing. Return to the oven for 10 minutes to heat through. Serve hot.

Note: If your portobello mushrooms don't have enough useable stems for adding to the stuffing, chop an additional portobello cap or a few white mushrooms to supplement (to equal about ½ cup).

Deconstructed Enchilada Bake

<$1.50 per serving

Makes 4 servings

When you're in the mood for enchiladas but short on time, try this quick and easy casserole for the same great flavors with less work.

1 tablespoon olive oil
¼ cup minced onion
2 garlic cloves, minced
¼ teaspoon chili powder
¼ teaspoon ground cumin
1½ cups cooked or 1 (15.5-ounce) can pinto beans, drained, rinsed, and mashed
2 tablespoons water

¼ teaspoon salt
Black pepper
1½ cups cooked or 1 (15.5-ounce) can black beans, drained, rinsed, and mashed
1 (24-ounce) jar tomato salsa
8 (7-inch) flour tortillas
½ cup Cheezee Sauce (page 36)

1 Heat the oil in a large skillet over medium-high heat. Add the onion, cover, and cook until softened, about 4 minutes. Add the garlic, chili powder, and cumin and cook, stirring, for 30 seconds. Add the pinto beans, water, salt, and pepper to taste. Cook, stirring frequently, until the flavors have blended and the mixture is well combined, about 5 minutes. Add the black beans and 1 cup of the salsa. Mix until combined. Set aside.

2 Preheat the oven to 350°F. Lightly oil a 9 × 13-inch baking pan. Spread a thin layer of the remaining salsa on the bottom of the prepared pan. Arrange half of the tortillas on top of the salsa, overlapping as necessary.

3 Spread the bean and salsa mixture over the tortillas in the baking pan, then top with the remaining tortillas. Spread the remaining salsa on top of the tortillas and drizzle with the cheezee sauce. Cover with foil and bake until hot and bubbly, about 30 minutes. Remove from oven and let stand for about 10 minutes before serving. Serve hot.

Variation

You could also use a round casserole dish and four large tortillas to make a layered casserole in the manner of the Tortilla Strata (page 156).

Splurge a Little

Top with shredded vegan cheddar cheese instead of the cheezee sauce.

Mexican Rice and Bean Bake

<$1.00 per serving

Makes 4 to 6 servings

The popular duo of rice and beans teams up well in this zesty casserole. The rice starts out on top of the stove, but finishes in the oven, so there's no standing around to watch pots.

1 tablespoon olive oil

1 medium onion, chopped

2 garlic cloves, minced

1 cup long-grain brown rice

1 teaspoon chili powder

2 cups water or vegetable stock
(page 45)

¼ teaspoon black pepper

Salt

1 (16-ounce) jar tomato salsa

3 cups cooked or 2 (15.5-ounce)
cans pinto beans, drained and
rinsed

1 (4-ounce) can mild diced green
chiles

1 cup fresh or thawed frozen corn
kernels (optional)

½ cup Cheezee Sauce (page 36;
optional)

❶ Preheat the oven to 350°F. Lightly oil a 9 × 13-inch baking pan and set aside.

❷ In a large saucepan, heat the oil over medium heat. Add the onion, cover, and cook until softened. Add the garlic and cook 30 seconds longer. Stir in the rice, chili powder, and water and bring to a boil. Turn off the heat and add the pepper and salt to taste. (The amount of salt you need will depend on if you use broth or water.)

❸ Carefully transfer the rice mixture to the prepared pan. Stir in the salsa, beans, chiles, and corn, if using. Cover tightly with foil and bake until the rice is tender and the water is absorbed, about 45 minutes.

❹ When the casserole is ready, remove it from the oven, uncover, and spread the cheezee sauce on top, if using. Return to the oven until heated through, about 10 minutes. Serve hot.

Splurge a Little

Top with vegan sour cream. Substitute shredded vegan cheddar cheese for the cheezee sauce.

Baked Ziti

<$1.50 per serving

Makes 4 to 6 servings

This old family favorite is an easy alternative to lasagna that also uses tofu in place of the ricotta cheese. It's a great make-ahead meal since it can be assembled in advance and popped in the oven at dinner time, freeing you to make a salad and set the table, or maybe just relax with a glass of wine. Use the Marinara Sauce on page 32 or your favorite bottled sauce.

12 ounces ziti	1½ teaspoons dried basil
3½ cups Marinara Sauce (page 32)	¾ teaspoon dried oregano
1 pound extra-firm tofu, drained	1 teaspoon salt
and crumbled	¼ teaspoon black pepper
3 tablespoons nutritional yeast	
¼ cup minced fresh parsley	

1 Preheat the oven to 350°F. Lightly oil a 3½-quart casserole and set aside.

2 In a large pot of boiling salted water, cook the ziti over medium-high heat, stirring occasionally, until al dente, about 10 minutes. Drain well and return to the pot. Add 2 cups of the marinara sauce and toss to coat.

3 In a large bowl, combine the tofu, yeast, parsley, basil, oregano, salt, and pepper. Taste and adjust the seasonings, if necessary.

4 Spread a thin layer of marinara sauce in the bottom of the prepared casserole. Add half of the pasta mixture and top with the tofu mixture. Top with the remaining pasta and spread the remaining marinara on top.

5 Cover tightly with foil and bake until hot, about 45 minutes. Serve hot.

Splurge a Little

Top with shredded vegan mozzarella and bake for an additional 10 minutes to melt. For convenience, use store-bought marinara sauce.

Cacciatore Noodle Bake

<$2.00 per serving

Makes 4 servings

While you can also serve this dish fresh from the stovetop, I like to combine everything in a casserole so I can assemble it in advance and then get the cleanup done while it does a short time in the oven. This also allows time for the delicious flavors to mingle.

8 ounces fettuccine, broken into thirds

1 tablespoon olive oil

8 ounces seitan (page 50), cut into ½-inch dice

1 medium yellow onion, chopped

1 medium green bell pepper, chopped

3 garlic cloves, minced

8 ounces small white mushrooms, lightly rinsed, patted dry, and quartered

1 teaspoon dried basil

½ teaspoon dried oregano

½ teaspoon sugar

½ teaspoon salt

¼ teaspoon black pepper

1 (28-ounce) can diced tomatoes, undrained

1 (14.5-ounce) can crushed tomatoes

❶ Preheat the oven to 375°F. Lightly oil a 9 × 13-inch baking pan or 3-quart casserole and set aside.

❷ In a large pot of boiling salted water, cook the fettuccine over medium-high heat, stirring occasionally, until al dente, about 10 minutes. Drain well and transfer to the prepared pan.

❸ In a large skillet, heat the oil over medium heat. Add the seitan and cook until browned all over, about 8 minutes. Add the seitan to the cooked fettuccine.

❹ Reheat the same skillet and add the onion, cover, and cook until softened, about 5 minutes. Add the bell pepper, garlic, and mushrooms, and cook 5 minutes longer. Stir in the basil, oregano, sugar, salt, and black pepper, then add the diced and crushed tomatoes, with their juice, stirring to blend. Add the tomato mixture to the pan with the fettuccine and seitan and toss to combine.

❺ Cover tightly with foil and bake for 30 minutes. Serve hot.

Deluxe Vegetable Lasagna

<$2.00 per serving

Makes 8 servings

Lasagna has the distinction of being one of the all-time greatest crowd-pleasers. When made with vegan ingredients, it can be economical as well. This recipe is for a large 9 x 13-inch lasagna pan, but if your "crowd" is limited to one or two people, you can still make the recipe; just divide it among two or even three smaller baking dishes, cutting the lasagna noodles to fit. Then freeze what you don't use. Adding vegetables to the lasagna in a variety of ways adds extra flavor, texture, and nutrition, and also turns the dish into an easy one-dish meal. Use the Marinara Sauce on page 32 or your favorite bottled sauce. Variation: Instead of the cauliflower topping, drizzle on some white sauce or Cheezee Sauce (page 36) instead.

2 medium zucchini (about 1½ pounds), cut lengthwise into ⅛-inch slices

1 tablespoon olive oil, plus more for roasting zucchini

Salt and black pepper

12 ounces lasagna noodles

2 pounds firm tofu, drained and mashed

½ cup nutritional yeast

¼ cup chopped fresh parsley

1½ teaspoons dried basil

½ teaspoon dried oregano

2 cups finely chopped white mushrooms

1 (10-ounce) bag frozen chopped spinach, thawed and squeezed dry

4 cups Marinara Sauce (page 32)

Cauliflower Topping (optional)

1½ cups steamed cauliflower

2 tablespoons nutritional yeast

½ teaspoon salt

¼ cup plain unsweetened soy milk

① Preheat the oven to 425°F. Lightly oil a baking sheet and arrange the zucchini slices on it in a single layer. Drizzle the zucchini with a little oil and season with salt and pepper to taste. Roast the zucchini until tender, about 10 minutes. Set aside to cool. Reduce the oven temperature to 350°F.

2 Place the noodles in a 9 × 13-inch baking pan and pour on enough boiling salted water to cover. Set aside while you make the filling.

3 In a large bowl, combine the tofu and yeast. Mash well to combine. Add the parsley, basil, oregano, 1 teaspoon of salt, and ½ teaspoon of pepper. Mix well to combine. Taste and adjust the seasonings, adding a pinch more salt if necessary.

4 In a large skillet, heat the oil over medium heat. Add the mushrooms and cook until they release their liquid, 3 to 4 minutes. Add the spinach and season with salt to taste. Cook until the liquid is absorbed. Set aside.

5 Drain and blot the noodles. Spread a layer of the marinara sauce in the bottom of the pan. Arrange 4 of the noodles on top of the sauce, slightly overlapping. Spread 1¼ cups of the tofu mixture over the noodles in a thin layer. Spread a layer of the zucchini slices on top of the noodles and top with half of the spinach-mushroom mixture.

6 Repeat layering with the sauce, noodles, tofu mixture, zucchini slices, and spinach-mushroom mixture, ending with noodles topped with marinara sauce.

7 Cover the lasagna with foil and bake 45 minutes.

8 **Make the cauliflower topping, if using:** Puree the cauliflower in a blender with the yeast and salt. Add as much of the soy milk as needed to make it a spreadable consistency. Uncover the lasagna and spread the cauliflower mixture on top. Return the lasagna to the oven and bake until hot and golden, 15 to 20 minutes longer. Let stand for 10 to 15 minutes to firm up. Serve hot.

Splurge a Little

Spread shredded vegan mozzarella cheese on top of the lasagna instead of the cauliflower mixture. For convenience, use store-bought marinara sauce.

Tempeh Bobotee

<$1.50 per serving

Makes 4 to 6 servings

Tempeh stands in for the meat in this flavorful and unusual South African casserole seasoned with curry and bits of apple, almonds, and raisins. It's terrific served with a little Cheapskate Chutney (page 39). For an even more economical version of this recipe, substitute seitan for the tempeh.

1 (12-ounce) package tempeh

1 tablespoon canola or other neutral oil

1 large yellow onion, chopped

1 tablespoon hot or mild curry powder

1 tablespoon light brown sugar

Salt and black pepper

1 slice white bread

1 cup plain unsweetened soy milk

½ cup coarsely ground raw almonds

¼ cup golden raisins or chopped dried apricots

1 cup chopped Granny Smith apple

2 tablespoons fresh lemon juice

1 cup crumbled firm tofu

1 tablespoon cornstarch

❶ Preheat the oven to 350°F. Lightly oil an 8-inch square baking pan and set aside.

❷ In a medium saucepan of simmering water, cook the tempeh for 30 minutes. Drain and cool, then grate or finely mince and set aside.

❸ In a large skillet, heat the oil over medium heat. Add the onion, cover, and cook until softened, about 5 minutes. Add the cooked tempeh. Stir in the curry powder, sugar, and salt and pepper to taste. Cook, stirring to coat, until the tempeh is golden brown, about 5 minutes. Set aside.

❹ Soak the bread in the soy milk. Squeeze the soy milk from the bread and reserve both separately.

❺ In a large bowl, combine the tempeh mixture with the bread, ¼ cup of the almonds, raisins, apple, and lemon juice, mixing well with your hands.

❻ In a blender or food processor, combine the reserved soy milk with the tofu, cornstarch, and ½ teaspoon of salt. Blend until smooth. Add the soy mixture to the other ingredients and mix well.

❼ Transfer the mixture to the prepared baking pan. Sprinkle the remaining ¼ cup almonds on top, cover tightly with foil, and bake for 45 minutes. Remove cover and bake 10 minutes longer to toast the almonds. Serve hot.

White Beans and Lemon Potatoes with Olives and Tomatoes

<$1.50 per serving

Makes 4 servings

Creamy beans and potatoes combine with the bright flavors of olives, lemon, and tomatoes, with fresh parsley adding a refreshing counterpoint. Sautéed spinach or another cooked vegetable makes a good addition and turns this into a budget-stretching one-dish meal.

1½ pounds small white or
    Yukon Gold potatoes, cut
    into 2-inch pieces
3 garlic cloves, crushed
Olive oil
Salt and black pepper
1½ cups cooked or 1 (15.5-ounce)
    can white beans, drained
    and rinsed

6 to 8 Oven-Dried Tomatoes
    (page 33), cut into ¼-inch strips
½ cup chopped fresh parsley
⅓ cup kalamata olives, pitted
    and chopped
Juice of 1 lemon

1 Preheat the oven to 400°F. Lightly oil a 9 × 13-inch baking pan. Add the potatoes and garlic, drizzle with a little oil, and season with salt and pepper to taste. Bake until tender, about 45 minutes.

2 Remove the potatoes from the oven and add the beans, tomatoes, parsley, olives, and lemon juice. Drizzle with a little more olive oil if needed to moisten and season with salt and pepper to taste. Toss to combine, then return to the oven to heat through, about 10 minutes. Serve hot.

Splurge a Little

Add an additional ¼ cup of olives. Add a tablespoon or so of capers. Use bottled sun-dried tomatoes packed in oil. Add cooked artichoke hearts.

Savory Vegetable Cobbler

Makes 6 servings

The yummy topping is like having built-in biscuits to sop up the rich sauce in this delicious cold weather one-dish meal.

Filling

8 ounces green beans, trimmed and cut into 1-inch pieces

2 tablespoons olive oil

1 medium yellow onion, chopped

2 medium carrots, cut into ¼-inch slices

1 large white potato, peeled and chopped

½ cup thinly sliced celery

8 ounces seitan (page 50), coarsely chopped

2 tablespoons chopped fresh parsley

1 teaspoon dried thyme

½ teaspoon dried sage

½ teaspoon dried marjoram

¼ teaspoon salt

¼ teaspoon black pepper

1 cup thawed frozen corn kernels

1 cup thawed frozen peas

Sauce

3 tablespoons vegan margarine

¼ cup all-purpose flour

1½ cups vegetable stock (page 45)

2 tablespoons soy sauce

1 cup plain unsweetened soy milk

Topping

2 cups all-purpose flour

2 teaspoons baking powder

1 teaspoon salt

2 tablespoons vegan margarine

1 cup plain unsweetened soy milk

❶ Preheat the oven to 400°F. Lightly oil a 9 × 13-inch baking pan and set aside.

❷ **Make the filling:** Steam the green beans until just tender, about 8 minutes. Set aside. In a large skillet, heat the oil over medium heat. Add the onion, carrots, potato, and celery, cover, and cook, until softened, about 7 minutes. Stir in the seitan, parsley, thyme, sage, marjoram, salt, and pepper. Cook, stirring, for 5 minutes, then stir in the corn, peas, and steamed green beans. Transfer the filling mixture to the prepared pan and set aside.

3 **Make the sauce:** In a medium saucepan, melt the margarine over medium heat. Add the flour, stirring to blend. Cook, stirring, for 3 minutes to cook out the raw taste of the flour. Stir in the stock, soy sauce, and soy milk and simmer, stirring constantly, until the sauce thickens, about 7 minutes. Add the sauce to the filling mixture and stir to combine. Set aside.

4 **Make the topping:** In a large bowl, combine the flour, baking powder, and salt. Use a pastry blender or fork to cut in the margarine until it resembles coarse crumbs. Add the soy milk to the mixture, stirring to form a stiff dough. (Add more soy milk if the dough is too dry.) Drop the dough mixture on top of the filling by the spoonful, smoothing a bit to evenly spread it about ½ inch thick. The top should look rustic and not come to the edge of the pan. Bake until the crust is golden brown and the filling is bubbling, about 30 minutes. Serve hot.

Variation

Instead of seitan, you could use extra-firm tofu or simmered tempeh.

Splurge a Little

Use fresh herbs instead of dried.

Vegetable Crisp

Makes 4 to 6 servings

Inspired by the delightful fruit crisps, this savory version also has a crunchy, crumbly topping. You can vary the ingredients according to what's in season or on sale. For example, if eggplant is expensive and zucchini is on sale, omit the eggplant and double the zucchini. If fresh basil is at a premium, use fresh parsley augmented by some dried basil. I prefer using a red bell pepper in this dish, but if they're too expensive, you can use a green one.

Vegetables

3 tablespoons olive oil

3 tablespoons sherry vinegar

3 garlic cloves, minced

3 tablespoons chopped fresh basil

$\frac{1}{2}$ teaspoon dried marjoram

$\frac{1}{2}$ teaspoon dried thyme

$\frac{1}{2}$ teaspoon salt

$\frac{1}{4}$ teaspoon black pepper

1 large red onion, halved lengthwise and sliced paper thin

1 large eggplant, peeled and cut into $\frac{1}{4}$-inch slices

3 medium zucchini, cut diagonally into $\frac{1}{4}$-inch slices

2 large portobello mushroom caps, cut into $\frac{1}{2}$-inch slices

2 large ripe tomatoes, cut into $\frac{1}{4}$-inch slices

Topping

1 cup fresh bread crumbs

2 tablespoons nutritional yeast

2 tablespoons chopped fresh parsley

1 teaspoon dried thyme

1 teaspoon dried basil

$\frac{1}{2}$ teaspoon dried marjoram

2 tablespoons olive oil

2 teaspoons fresh lemon juice

$\frac{1}{4}$ teaspoon salt

$\frac{1}{4}$ teaspoon black pepper

❶ **Make the vegetables:** Preheat the oven to 425°F. In a small bowl, whisk together the oil, vinegar, garlic, basil, marjoram, thyme, salt, and pepper.

❷ Place the onion, eggplant, zucchini, and mushrooms on baking sheets and brush with the oil-vinegar mixture on both sides. The vegetables can overlap slightly, but keep each type of vegetable separate. Bake until softened, about 15 minutes.

❸ Make the topping: In a medium bowl, combine all the topping ingredients, stirring to mix well.

❹ Lightly oil a 9-inch square baking pan or 2-quart gratin dish. When the vegetables are finished roasting, remove from the oven, and set aside until cool enough to handle. Reduce the oven temperature to 375°F.

❺ Arrange a layer of the eggplant slices on the bottom of the prepared pan; top with a layer of onion, followed by the mushrooms, zucchini, and the tomatoes. Drizzle with any remaining oil-vinegar mixture and repeat the layering until all the vegetables are used. Sprinkle the topping mixture over vegetables. Bake until hot, about 30 minutes. Serve immediately.

Splurge a Little

Use fresh herbs instead of dried. Add a layer of cooked, sliced artichoke hearts.

Rice Island Casserole

<$1.00 per serving

Makes 4 to 6 servings

Island flavors permeate this rice and bean bake with bits of pineapple and coconut adding a surprise sweetness and a minced chile adding heat. Serve with a cooked green vegetable on the side to complete the meal.

1 tablespoon canola or other neutral oil

1 hot red or green chile, seeded and minced

3 garlic cloves, minced

½ cup chopped green onions

1 large carrot, shredded

1 cup long-grain brown rice

2 tablespoons soy sauce

1 teaspoon ground cumin

¾ teaspoon dried thyme

½ teaspoon ground allspice

½ teaspoon salt

¼ teaspoon black pepper

2 cups vegetable stock (page 45)

1½ cups cooked or 1 (15.5-ounce) can dark red kidney beans, drained and rinsed

1 (8-ounce) can crushed pineapple, undrained

¼ cup unsweetened shredded coconut

3 tablespoons chopped fresh cilantro

2 tablespoons chopped unsalted roasted cashews

❶ Preheat the oven to 375°F. Lightly oil a 2-quart gratin dish and set aside.

❷ In a large saucepan, heat the oil over medium heat. Add the chile, garlic, green onions, and carrot. Cook, stirring, to soften for 1 minute. Stir in the rice, soy sauce, cumin, thyme, allspice, salt, and pepper. Stir in the stock and bring to a boil. Reduce to a simmer and cook for 10 minutes to soften the rice and blend the flavors.

❸ Transfer the mixture to the prepared gratin dish. Add the beans, pine-apple, and coconut. Taste and adjust seasonings, if necessary. Mix well to combine, then cover tightly with foil and bake until the rice is tender, about 1 hour. If all the liquid is not absorbed, return to the oven uncovered and bake for a few minutes more. Fluff the rice with a fork, sprinkle with the cilantro and cashews, and serve.

Spinach Pie

<$1.00 per serving

Makes 6 servings to 8

Even when quiche was in its prime and not just retro, my husband Jon had an aversion to it. So, in my house, I make what I simply call "spinach pie" and the "q" word never gets mentioned. Frozen spinach works great in this recipe and is more economical than fresh, which you can use instead if you're feeling flush.

½ recipe Double Pie Crust
   (page 59)
2 tablespoons olive oil
1 medium sweet yellow onion,
   minced
2 garlic cloves, minced
1 cup chopped white mushrooms
1 (10-ounce) package frozen
   chopped spinach, thawed
1 teaspoon dried savory
½ teaspoon turmeric

¼ teaspoon ground nutmeg
1 teaspoon salt
¼ teaspoon black pepper
½ cup unsalted raw cashews
¼ cup plain unsweetened soy milk
2 tablespoons nutritional yeast
1 tablespoon cornstarch
1 teaspoon yellow or spicy brown
   mustard
1 pound extra-firm tofu, drained

1 Preheat the oven to 400°F. Roll out the dough between two sheets of lightly floured plastic wrap. Fit the crust into the bottom of a 9-inch pie plate or quiche pan, crimping the edges. Bake the crust for 10 minutes, then remove from oven. Set aside. Reduce the oven temperature to 350°F.

2 In a large skillet, heat the oil over medium heat. Add the onion, cover, and cook until softened, about 5 minutes. Add the garlic and mushrooms and cook 1 minute longer. Stir in the spinach, savory, turmeric, nutmeg, salt, and pepper. Cook for 5 minutes, stirring occasionally. Set aside.

3 In a high-speed blender, grind the cashews into fine crumbs. Add the soy milk, yeast, cornstarch, and mustard and blend until smooth. Squeeze any remaining water out of the tofu and add it to the cashew mixture. Blend until smooth. Spoon about half of the spinach mixture into the tofu mixture and pulse to combine.

4 Transfer the tofu-spinach mixture to a large bowl and add the remaining spinach mixture. Stir well to combine. Taste and adjust seasonings, adding more salt if necessary.

5 Spread the mixture evenly into the prepared pie crust. Bake until the edges of the crust are lightly browned, about 45 minutes. Let it sit for at least 15 minutes before serving. Serve warm or at room temperature.

Torta Rustica

<$1.00 per serving

Makes 8 servings

If you're looking for an interesting and delicious recipe to serve guests, this is a good choice. It has a long ingredient list, but if you have pie dough and vegan sausage on hand, the recipe goes together quickly and is an inexpensive way to put a special meal on the table. If you don't like eggplant, substitute sliced zucchini.

2 medium eggplants, cut into ¼-inch slices

2 tablespoons olive oil

1 medium yellow onion, chopped

3 garlic cloves, minced

8 ounces white mushrooms, chopped

8 ounces finely chopped Close to Mom's Sausage Patties (page 54) or Big Stick Pepperoni (page 56)

1 teaspoon dried basil

½ teaspoon dried marjoram

½ teaspoon dried oregano

½ teaspoon salt

½ teaspoon black pepper

¼ teaspoon crushed red pepper

2 (10-ounce) packages frozen chopped spinach, thawed and well drained

1½ cups cooked or 1 (15.5-ounce) can cannellini beans, drained and rinsed

¼ cup nutritional yeast

1 (14.5-ounce) can diced tomatoes, drained

1 (9-ounce) jar roasted bell peppers, drained and finely chopped

2 tablespoons chopped fresh parsley

1 recipe Double Pie Crust (page 59)

❶ Preheat the oven to 425°F. Brush the eggplant slices with 1 tablespoon oil and bake for 10 minutes on each side. Set aside to cool. Reduce the oven temperature to 400°F.

❷ In a large skillet, heat the remaining 1 tablespoon of oil over medium heat. Add the onion, cover, and cook until softened, about 10 minutes. Uncover, stir in the garlic, mushrooms, sausage, basil, marjoram, oregano, salt, black pepper, and crushed red pepper. Cook until softened, stirring occasionally, about 10 minutes. Stir in the spinach and cook until all the liquid is evaporated, about 5 minutes. Set aside to cool completely.

❸ In a food processor, combine the beans and yeast and process until smooth. Set aside.

❹ In a medium bowl, combine the tomatoes, roasted peppers, and parsley. Mix well and set aside.

5 You want the bottom crust to be larger than the top, so if your pieces of dough are equal in size, cut about one third of the dough from the piece to be used for the top and add it to the dough for the bottom. Roll out the dough for the bottom crust between two sheets of lightly floured plastic wrap or parchment paper until the dough is about 14 inches in diameter. Place the crust into a 9-inch springform pan, pressing the dough against the sides of the pan and letting the edge of the dough hang over the edge of the pan.

6 Spread a layer of the bean mixture on the bottom crust. Top with a layer of eggplant, followed by the sausage-spinach mixture, and the tomato-pepper mixture. Repeat the layering until all the ingredients are used up.

7 Roll out the remaining dough for the top crust between two sheets of lightly floured plastic wrap and place it on top of the filling. Crimp together the edges of the top and bottom crusts to seal the edges. Make 4 small slits in the top to let steam escape.

8 Place the pan on a baking sheet or wrap the bottom of the pan with foil. Bake until the crust is golden brown, about 45 minutes. Cool the torta in the pan for at least 30 minutes. Remove the sides of the pan and serve warm or at room temperature.

Samosa Pie

Makes 6 servings

When you're in the mood for samosas but don't have time to make them, try this luscious pie that transforms the savory Indian appetizer into a gorgeous one-dish meal. If great taste and good looks weren't enough, it's also easy to prepare.

1 pound baking potatoes, peeled
   and cut into 1-inch dice
8 ounces green beans, trimmed and
   cut into ½-inch pieces
½ recipe Double Pie Crust
   (page 59)
1 tablespoon canola or other
   neutral oil
1 large yellow onion, finely chopped
1 medium carrot, finely chopped
1 teaspoon grated fresh ginger

1 tablespoon hot or mild curry
   powder
½ teaspoon ground coriander
½ teaspoon salt
¼ teaspoon ground cumin
¼ teaspoon ground cayenne
1½ cups cooked or 1 (15.5-ounce)
   can chickpeas, drained
   and rinsed
1 cup thawed frozen peas

1 Steam the potatoes until just tender, about 12 minutes. Set aside. Steam the green beans until just tender, about 8 minutes. Set aside. Preheat the oven to 400°F.

2 Roll out the dough between two sheets of lightly floured plastic wrap. Fit the crust into the bottom of a 9-inch pie plate or quiche pan, crimping the edges. Bake the crust for 10 minutes, then remove from the oven. Set aside. Reduce the oven temperature to 350°F.

3 In a large skillet, heat the oil over medium heat. Add the onion and carrot, cover, and cook until soft, about 7 minutes. Stir in the ginger, curry powder, coriander, salt, cumin, and cayenne. Remove from the heat. Add the steamed potatoes and chickpeas, stirring to mix well and mash the potatoes and chickpeas coarsely. Add the peas and steamed green beans, stirring to mix well. Taste and adjust the seasonings, if necessary.

4 Spread the filling mixture evenly into the prepared pie crust. Bake until the filling is hot and golden and the crust is browned, about 45 minutes. Serve hot.

Pizza, Burgers, and Sandwiches

*B*y a happy coincidence, sometimes our favorite meals also happen to be easy and cheap. Who doesn't love a great burger, fresh hot pizza, or a tasty sandwich? When paired with a simple salad, a vegetable side dish, or a bowl of hot soup, you've got an arsenal of great and inexpensive mealtime options.

Whether you're looking for wholesome and economical alternatives to fast-food meals or ways to feed a houseful of hungry teenagers, this chapter is loaded with great-tasting sandwiches such as Smoky Joes (page 184) and Cajun-Spiced Seitan Po' Boys (page 181), as well as a selection of burritos, fajitas, and wraps. Burger fans will enjoy Very Veggie Burgers (page 179) and Better Bean Burgers (page 178), along with their numerous variations. Sandwiches and burgers can be especially thrifty when you avoid those expensive meat and cheese alternatives and make your own.

Homemade pizza can be fun to make and certainly more economical than ordering out. There's a sensational Pepperoni-Mushroom Pizza on page 190 with lots of variations that will satisfy the pizza lovers in your house, as well as the less familiar but equally delicious Tuscan White Bean Pizza (page 192) and Polenta Pizza with Roasted Vegetables (page 194).

When you keep tortillas on hand and extra bread and pizza dough in the freezer, easy and satisfying meals are always within reach.

Better Bean Burgers

<$1.00 per serving

Makes 4 servings

When you can make quick and easy homemade burgers like this, there's no need to spend the money for ready-made burgers. Best of all, you can season these any way you'd like, adding different herbs or spices, such as cumin and cilantro, to suit your taste.

1½ cups cooked or 1 (15.5-ounce) can black beans, drained and rinsed

3 tablespoons wheat gluten flour (vital wheat gluten)

½ cup dry bread crumbs

¼ cup minced red onion

2 tablespoons minced fresh parsley

½ teaspoon salt

¼ teaspoon black pepper

2 tablespoons olive oil

4 burger rolls

Condiments of choice

1 Place the beans in a medium bowl and mash well. Sprinkle the flour on the beans and mix well to combine. Add the bread crumbs, onion, parsley, salt, and pepper. Mix well. Use your hands to shape the mixture into 4 patties, no more than ¼ inch thick. Set aside.

2 In a large skillet, heat the oil over medium heat. Add the burgers, cover, and cook for 5 minutes. Uncover, use a spatula to flip the burgers, and cook, uncovered, for 5 minutes more.

3 Serve on burger rolls with your favorite condiments.

Very Veggie Burgers

<$1.00 per serving

Makes 4 servings

These tasty burgers are a great way to use up leftover mashed potatoes. If you don't have any mashers on hand, you can quickly "bake" a potato in the microwave (on High for 6 to 8 minutes) and scoop out the center to use in this recipe. Serve on your favorite burger rolls with all the trimmings or eat them on a plate topped with a gravy or sauce such as Creamy Mushroom Gravy (page 31) or Cheezee Sauce (page 36).

2 tablespoons olive oil

½ cup chopped onion

2 garlic cloves, minced

1 cup chopped white mushrooms

2 green onions, chopped

⅓ cup shredded carrot

1 cup cooked mashed potatoes (see headnote)

3 tablespoons dry bread crumbs

3 tablespoons ground unsalted roasted cashews

1 tablespoon chopped fresh parsley

2 teaspoons chopped fresh basil

½ teaspoon salt

¼ teaspoon black pepper

1 In a large skillet, heat 1 tablespoon of the oil over medium heat. Add the onion, cover, and cook until softened, about 5 minutes. Stir in the garlic, mushrooms, green onions, and carrot and cook until the vegetables are softened and any liquid is absorbed, about 5 minutes more.

2 Transfer the onion mixture to a large bowl. Add the potatoes, bread crumbs, cashews, parsley, basil, salt, and pepper. Mix well to combine. Use your hands to shape the mixture into 4 patties, about ¼ inch thick.

3 In a large skillet, heat the remaining 1 tablespoon oil over medium heat. Add the patties and cook, turning once until golden brown on both sides, 4 to 5 minutes per side. Serve hot.

Lemony Garlic Chickpea Patties

<$1.00 per serving

Makes 4 servings

Stuffed into pita pockets, these tasty patties are a protein-packed Middle Eastern feast. Instead of pita, you can use them in a wrap or on a roll. You can even serve them on a plate as a main dish, topped with your favorite sauce or gravy. I enjoy them topped with a spoonful of Skordalia (page 99) or Handy Hummus (page 44).

4 garlic cloves, crushed

3 tablespoons chopped fresh parsley or cilantro

2 green onions, coarsely chopped

1½ cups cooked or 1 (15.5-ounce) can chickpeas, drained and rinsed

1 cup dry bread crumbs

3 tablespoons wheat gluten flour (vital wheat gluten)

3 tablespoons fresh lemon juice

½ teaspoon salt

¼ teaspoon black pepper

1 tablespoon olive oil

4 (7-inch) pita breads

1 cup shredded romaine or iceberg lettuce

1 medium ripe tomato, cut into ¼-inch slices

Handy Hummus (page 44) or Skordalia (page 99; optional)

❶ In a food processor, combine the garlic, parsley, green onions, and chickpeas, and pulse to combine. Add the bread crumbs, flour, lemon juice, salt, and pepper. Pulse to mix, leaving some texture. Shape the mixture into 4 patties and set aside.

❷ In a large skillet, heat the oil over medium heat. Place the patties in the hot skillet. Cook until golden brown on both sides, turning once, 4 to 5 minutes per side.

❸ To serve, stuff the patties into the pita pockets along with the lettuce and tomato. Spoon on some hummus or skordalia, if using.

Cajun-Spiced Seitan Po' Boys

<$1.00 per serving

Makes 4 servings

The famous New Orleans sandwich takes a decidedly vegan turn with a yummy seitan filling, seasoned with Cajun spices and Creole mustard. Add the optional sliced jalapeños if you like more heat, or simply splash on some Tabasco sauce.

2 tablespoons olive oil

1 large red onion, cut into ¼-inch slices

8 ounces seitan (page 50), sliced very thin

Cajun seasoning

Salt and black pepper

1 French baguette or 4 small sub rolls

4 tablespoons Creole mustard

2 cups shredded romaine or iceberg lettuce

1 large ripe tomato, cut into ¼-inch slices

Pickled sliced jalapeños (optional)

1 In a large skillet, heat 1 tablespoon of the oil over medium heat. Add the onion, cover, and cook until softened, about 5 minutes. Uncover and cook until golden brown, about 5 minutes more. Scoop the onions out of the skillet and set aside.

2 Return the same skillet to the stove over medium heat. Add the remaining 1 tablespoon oil and heat until hot. Sprinkle the seitan slices with the Cajun seasoning to taste, and add to the skillet. Cook until browned on both sides, turning once. Return the onions to the skillet and cook until hot, sprinkling on additional Cajun seasoning, if desired, and salt and pepper to taste. Set aside.

3 If using a baguette, cut it into 4 equal pieces. To assemble the sandwiches, slice the baguette portions or rolls and slather Creole mustard on the inside top and bottom. Spread some lettuce onto the bottom of each sandwich, followed by the tomato slices. Top with the seitan slices and a few slices of jalapeño, if using. Serve at once.

Roasted Vegetable Sandwiches with Creamy White Bean Spread

<$1.50 per serving

Makes 4 servings

These open-faced sandwiches make a sophisticated and flavorful lunch. They're also great as part of a light dinner with a bowl of soup.

1 large red onion, cut into ¼-inch slices

1 portobello mushroom cap, lightly rinsed, patted dry, and cut into ¼-inch strips

2 medium zucchini, cut into ¼-inch slices

1 tablespoon olive oil, plus more for roasting vegetables

Salt and black pepper

2 garlic cloves, minced

1½ cups cooked or 1 (15.5-ounce) can cannellini beans, drained and rinsed

2 tablespoons sherry vinegar

½ teaspoon crushed red pepper

2 tablespoons chopped fresh basil or parsley

8 (½-inch-thick) slices Italian bread, toasted

❶ Preheat the oven to 425°F. Lightly oil a baking sheet. Arrange the onion, mushroom, and zucchini on the baking sheet. Drizzle with oil and season with salt and pepper to taste. Roast until tender and slightly browned on the edges, turning once, about 20 minutes.

❷ Heat the remaining tablespoon of oil in a large skillet over medium heat. Add the garlic and cook until fragrant, about 30 seconds. Add the beans, vinegar, crushed red pepper, and basil. Season with salt and pepper to taste, and cook for 3 minutes to blend the flavors. Transfer the bean mixture to a food processor and process until smooth.

❸ To serve, spread the bean mixture evenly on each slice of toasted bread and top with some of the roasted vegetables. Arrange on plates, allowing 2 slices of bread per person.

Splurge a Little

Use an aged balsamic vinegar instead of the sherry vinegar.

Add a few leaves of fresh arugula to the sandwiches.

Curried Tofu Wraps

<$2.00 per serving

Makes 4 servings

Celery, nuts, and raisins provide texture and a slather of chutney adds a touch of spicy-sweet flavor to these protein-rich wraps. The optional cooked brown rice makes a tasty and nutritious addition. If wraps aren't your thing, try the mixture tucked into pita pockets, on toasted bread, or spooned directly on the plate.

1 tablespoon canola or other neutral oil

1 pound extra-firm tofu, drained and crumbled

1 tablespoon plus 1 teaspoon hot or mild curry powder

Salt and black pepper

¾ cup minced celery

¼ cup finely chopped unsalted roasted cashews or peanuts

¼ cup golden raisins

2 tablespoons chopped fresh parsley

1 tablespoon minced green onion

½ cup Make-Your-Own Mayo (page 41)

1 teaspoon yellow mustard

1 cup cooked brown rice (optional)

½ cup Cheapskate Chutney (page 39)

4 (10-inch) flour tortillas

2 cups shredded romaine or iceberg lettuce

① In a large skillet, heat the oil over medium heat. Add the tofu and cook, stirring, until heated through, about 5 minutes. Sprinkle with the 1 tablespoon curry powder and salt and pepper to taste, and stir to combine. Transfer the tofu mixture to a large bowl. Add the celery, cashews, raisins, parsley, and green onion. Set aside.

② In a small bowl, combine the mayonnaise, mustard, and remaining 1 teaspoon curry powder. Stir to blend well, then add to the tofu mixture and stir to mix thoroughly. Stir in the rice, if using.

③ To assemble, spread a thin line of chutney down the center of a tortilla, then spoon one-quarter of the tofu mixture on top, followed by shredded lettuce. Roll up tightly and arrange on a plate. Repeat with remaining ingredients. Serve at once.

Splurge a Little

For convenience, use bottled chutney and vegan mayo.

Smoky Joes

<$1.00
per serving

Makes 4 servings

I like to use seitan to make this spicy version of sloppy joes, but you can also use frozen crumbled tofu, grated tempeh, or cooked bulgur to good effect.

8 ounces seitan (page 50)
1 tablespoon olive oil
½ cup minced onion
½ cup minced green bell pepper
2 garlic cloves, minced
1 tablespoon soy sauce
½ cup ketchup
1 tablespoon tomato paste
¼ cup water

1 or 2 chipotle chiles in adobo,
   finely minced
1 teaspoon brown mustard
1 tablespoon chili powder
½ teaspoon smoked paprika
½ teaspoon liquid smoke
½ teaspoon salt
¼ teaspoon black pepper
4 burger rolls

❶ Shred or finely chop the seitan and set it aside.

❷ In a large saucepan, heat the oil over medium heat. Add the onion and bell pepper, cover, and cook until softened, about 10 minutes. Add the garlic and cook 30 seconds longer. Stir in the chopped seitan and the soy sauce and cook for 2 to 3 minutes to lightly brown.

❸ Stir in the ketchup, tomato paste, water, chipotle, mustard, chili powder, paprika, liquid smoke, salt, and pepper. Mix well, adding a little more water if the mixture is too dry. Simmer for 5 minutes to blend flavors.

❹ When ready to serve, spoon the mixture onto the rolls and serve hot.

Wheatball Sandwiches

Makes 4 servings

These yummy sandwiches can be served on burger or kaiser rolls, if you prefer, in which case you would only need about 12 wheatballs. The actual number needed depends on how large you've made them and how stuffed you want your sandwiches to be.

12 to 16 Wheatballs (page 57)
2 cups Marinara Sauce (page 32)
⅓ cup Cheezee Sauce (page 36)

4 small sub rolls or other
    sandwich rolls

1. In a large saucepan, combine the wheatballs and marinara sauce, and heat over medium heat. Use a potato ricer to smash and flatten the balls, retaining some shape and texture. Cook stirring, until heated through, about 5 minutes. Keep warm. Preheat the broiler.

2. Heat the cheezee sauce in a small saucepan and keep warm.

3. Split the sub rolls and place them, cut side up, on a baking sheet. Toast the rolls, then arrange them on plates.

4. Divide the wheatball mixture among the rolls and drizzle each with some of the cheezee sauce. Serve hot.

Splurge a Little

For convenience, use a bottled marinara sauce and shredded vegan mozzarella cheese instead of the cheezee sauce.

Salsa Tofu Burritos

<$1.00 per serving

Makes 4 servings

These quick and easy burritos are a great way to enjoy your tofu and burritos, too.

1 tablespoon olive oil

1 pound extra-firm tofu, drained and crumbled

1 tablespoon nutritional yeast

1 tablespoon soy sauce

1 teaspoon hot sauce

Salt and black pepper

1 cup tomato salsa

4 (10-inch) flour tortillas

1 In a large skillet, heat the oil over medium heat. Add the tofu and sprinkle with the yeast, soy sauce, hot sauce, and salt and pepper to taste.

2 Stir in ½ cup of the salsa and continue cooking until hot.

3 To assemble burritos, spoon one-quarter of the mixture onto a tortilla, top with one-quarter of the remaining salsa, and roll up tightly. Repeat with the remaining ingredients and serve.

Splurge a Little

Add chopped avocado or shredded vegan cheese when assembling the burritos.

Bean and Cheezee Rice Burritos

<$1.50 per serving

Makes 4 servings

When you need to stretch a small amount of rice into a satisfying meal for four, try these yummy burritos. If you have some cheezee sauce already made, these go together in a flash.

1½ cups cooked or 1 (15.5-ounce) can pinto beans, drained and rinsed
½ cup tomato salsa
1 teaspoon chili powder
¼ cup canned chopped hot or mild green chiles
2 cups hot cooked rice

1 cup Cheezee Sauce (page 36)
4 (10-inch) flour tortillas
½ cup minced fresh ripe tomato
3 tablespoons minced red onion
2 tablespoons minced fresh cilantro (optional)
Hot sauce (optional)

1 In a medium saucepan, coarsely mash the beans over medium heat. Stir in the salsa, chili powder, and chiles and heat until hot, about 5 minutes.

2 In a medium bowl, combine the rice and ½ cup of the cheezee sauce, stirring to combine.

3 To assemble burritos, spoon a line of the rice mixture down each of the tortillas, top with a line of the bean mixture, then drizzle with a spoonful of the remaining cheezee sauce. Sprinkle with the tomato and onion and the cilantro and hot sauce, if using. Roll up tightly and serve hot.

Variation

Quesadillas: If you'd rather fold than roll, use the same ingredients to make Bean and Rice Quesadillas—just layer the ingredients on half of each tortilla, fold over, and heat in a medium-hot skillet or on a griddle until hot, turning once.

Build-Your-Own Fajitas

<$2.00 per serving

Makes 4 servings

Set out bowls of ingredients on the table and let everyone make their own fajitas. It's less work for you, plus it's more fun—and everyone can have it the way they like it. In addition to being a great family meal, this is an easy and economical idea for a teenager get-together as well. If you're serving a crowd, just double up on the ingredients. Place a bowl of corn chips and additional toppings, such as chopped kalamata olives, minced green onions, vegan sour cream, and hot sauce, on the table as well.

2 tablespoons olive oil

8 ounces seitan (page 50), cut into
  ½-inch strips

1 teaspoon chili powder

Salt and black pepper

1 large portobello mushroom cap,
  lightly rinsed, patted dry, and
  cut into ½-inch strips

1 large red onion, halved
  lengthwise and cut into
  ¼-inch slices

4 (10-inch) or 8 (6-inch) flour
  tortillas

1 green bell pepper, cut into
  ¼-inch strips

1½ cups tomato salsa

1 cup Cheapamole (page 35)

½ cup Cheezee Sauce (page 36),
  warmed

Additional toppings (see
  headnote)

1 Preheat the oven to 275°F. In a large skillet, heat 1 tablespoon of the oil over medium-high heat. Add the seitan and season with ½ teaspoon of the chili powder and salt and black pepper to taste. Cook until browned, then remove from the skillet and spoon onto a heatproof platter. Keep warm in the oven while you prepare the remaining ingredients.

2 Add the portobello strips to the same skillet over medium heat. Season with the remaining ½ teaspoon chili powder and salt and black pepper to taste. Cook, turning to coat, until the mushrooms are tender, about 5 minutes. Spoon alongside the seitan on the platter and return to the oven to keep warm.

3 Heat the remaining 1 tablespoon of oil in the same skillet over medium heat. Add the onion and season with salt and pepper to taste. Cook, stirring, until tender and golden brown, about 10 minutes. Arrange the onions next to the mushrooms on the platter and return to the oven to keep warm. Wrap the tortillas in foil and place them in the oven to warm.

4 Add the bell pepper to the same skillet over medium heat and cook, stirring, until softened, about 5 minutes. Arrange the cooked peppers next to the onions and return to the oven while you get the remaining ingredients assembled.

5 To serve, place the salsa and cheapamole in separate bowls and arrange on the table along with a bowl containing the warmed cheezee sauce and other desired accompaniments. Place the warmed tortillas on the table along with the platter containing the seitan and other fajita fillings. Serve at once.

Splurge a Little

Include avocado and store-bought vegan sour cream among the toppings. Use a red bell pepper instead of a green one.

Pepperoni-
Mushroom Pizza

<$1.00
per serving

Makes 1 (12-inch) pizza

When money is tight, the fantastic flavor and moderate cost of pizza can be the ideal dinner solution. Everyone loves it, it feeds a crowd, and it's fun to make. And unless you live in a metropolitan area, ordering a vegan pizza from a restaurant may be a pipe dream anyway. With this recipe you can include your favorite toppings—even pepperoni! Since pizza dough can be made in advance, it's a good idea to have some on hand for busy nights—just remember to take it out of the freezer for a few hours before needed so it can thaw and come to room temperature.

Dough
2¾ cups all-purpose flour
2¼ teaspoons instant yeast
1 teaspoon salt
1 cup lukewarm water

Topping
1 tablespoon olive oil
1 cup sliced Big Stick Pepperoni
   (page 56)
1 cup sliced white mushrooms
1 cup Marinara Sauce (page 32)
½ teaspoon dried oregano

1 **Make the dough:** In a large bowl, combine the flour, yeast, and salt. Stir in the water until combined, then use your hands to knead it into a soft dough.

2 Transfer the dough to a lightly floured work surface and knead until it is smooth and elastic, about 10 minutes. Shape the dough into a smooth ball and place in an oiled bowl. Cover with plastic wrap and let rise in a warm spot until doubled in size, about 1 hour.

3 After the dough has risen, transfer it to a lightly floured work surface, punch it down, and gently stretch and lift it to make a 12-inch round about ¼ inch thick. Transfer the round to a lightly floured baking sheet or pizza stone. Use your fingertips to form a rim around the perimeter of the dough and let rise in a draft-free place for 20 minutes. Adjust the oven rack to the bottommost position of the oven. Preheat oven to 425°F.

4 **Make the topping:** In a medium skillet, heat the oil over low heat. Add the pepperoni and mushrooms and cook, turning once, until softened, about 5 minutes. Set aside to cool.

⑤ To assemble the pizza, spread the marinara sauce on top of the dough round, to within ½ inch of the edge. Sprinkle with oregano and arrange the cooked pepperoni and mushrooms on top. Bake until the crust is browned, about 15 minutes. Serve hot.

Splurge a Little

Top with shredded vegan mozzarella cheese. Include other tasty toppings such as sliced artichoke hearts, imported pitted olives, or capers. For convenience, use store-bought vegan pepperoni.

Pizza Party

Why spend money on takeout pizza when you can make your own for a fraction of the cost? Use the recipe for Pepperoni-Mushroom Pizza (opposite page) or Tuscan White Bean Pizza (page 192) as a starting point and include your own favorite toppings. Let everyone help with the assembly. Depending on how many people you're feeding and what else you might be serving (such as a salad), you can put an extra pizza in the oven to bake while you're enjoying the first one. That way, every slice of pizza is hot and fresh.

Tuscan White Bean Pizza

<$1.00 per serving

Makes 1 (12-inch) pizza

The people of Tuscany come by the moniker "bean eaters" owing to their inclusion of *fagioli* in everything from soups and stews to this creamy, protein-rich pizza topping that will help you forget all about mozzarella cheese.

Dough

2¾ cups all-purpose flour

2¼ teaspoons instant yeast

1 teaspoon salt

1 cup lukewarm water

Topping

1 tablespoon olive oil

3 garlic cloves, finely minced

1½ cups cooked or 1 (15.5-ounce) can cannellini beans, drained and rinsed

¼ teaspoon salt

¼ teaspoon black pepper

⅓ cup water or vegetable stock (page 45)

3 tablespoons chopped fresh basil

2 medium ripe Roma tomatoes, cut into ¼-inch slices

1 Make the dough: In a large bowl, combine the flour, yeast, and salt. Stir in the water until combined, then use your hands to knead it into a soft dough.

2 Transfer the dough to a lightly floured work surface and knead until it is smooth and elastic, about 10 minutes, adding additional flour as needed so it doesn't stick. Shape the dough into a smooth ball and place in an oiled bowl. Cover with plastic wrap and let rise at room temperature in a warm spot until doubled in volume, about 1 hour.

3 After the dough has risen, transfer it to a lightly floured work surface, punch it down, and gently stretch and lift it to make a 12-inch round about ¼ inch thick. Transfer the round to a floured baking sheet or pizza stone. Let the dough rise in a draft-free place for 20 minutes. Adjust the oven rack to the bottommost position of the oven. Preheat oven to 425°F.

④ Make the topping: In a large skillet, heat the oil over medium heat. Add the garlic and cook until softened, about 2 minutes. Add the beans, salt, and pepper.

⑤ Mash the beans to break them up, then stir in the water and simmer, stirring occasionally, until the mixture is creamy, about 8 minutes. Stir in the basil and set aside.

⑥ To assemble the pizza, spread the bean mixture evenly on top of the dough round, to within ½ inch of the edge. Arrange the tomato slices on top and season with salt and pepper to taste. Bake until the crust is browned, 12 to 15 minutes. Serve hot.

Splurge a Little

Add sliced pitted kalamata olives when you add the tomatoes. Garnish with thin strips of fresh basil leaves.

Polenta Pizza with Roasted Vegetables

<$1.00
per serving

Makes 4 servings

Polenta makes a satisfying if nontraditional crust for pizza. Vary the toppings according to your personal taste, adding some vegan mozzarella cheese or pepperoni if desired. While the polenta does firm up nicely, it's not as sturdy as regular pizza crust, so you will probably want to "knife and fork" it rather than trying to eat a slice out of hand.

½ red onion, cut into ¼-inch slices
1 small zucchini, halved lengthwise and cut into ¼-inch slices
2 portobello mushroom caps, lightly rinsed, patted dry, and cut into ¼-inch slices
2 tablespoons olive oil

½ teaspoon dried oregano
Salt and black pepper
3 cups water
1 cup yellow cornmeal
1 cup Marinara Sauce (page 32)

❶ Preheat the oven to 425°F. Lightly oil a baking sheet and arrange the onion, zucchini, and mushrooms on it in a single layer. Drizzle with 1 tablespoon of the oil and season with oregano and salt and pepper to taste. Roast the vegetables until tender and lightly browned on the edges, turning once, about 20 minutes total. Set aside. Reduce the oven temperature to 375°F.

❷ In a large saucepan, combine the water, 1 teaspoon salt, and the remaining 1 tablespoon oil, and bring to a boil. Add the cornmeal, stirring constantly with a wire whisk. Reduce the heat to medium and cook, stirring frequently, until thickened, 12 to 15 minutes.

❸ Lightly oil a pizza pan or 9 × 13-inch baking pan. As soon as the polenta is cooked, spread it quickly in the prepared pan, using the back of a large spoon to spread it evenly to the ends of the pan. It should be about ¼ inch thick. Bake until firm, about 12 minutes.

❹ Spread the marinara sauce evenly over the crust, to within ½ inch of the edge. Arrange the roasted vegetables on top. Bake until hot, about 10 minutes. Serve hot.

Variations

Instead of the roasted vegetables, top the polenta with any of the following toppings:

- Salsa and a drizzle of Cheezee Sauce (page 36)
- Caramelized onions sprinkled with Smoky Tempeh Bits (page 58)
- Spinach (or other greens) sautéed with white beans in olive oil and garlic.
- Your favorite chili (Black and White Bean Chili, page 78, or French Lentil Chili, page 79, are good choices.)

Splurge a Little

Add additional toppings such as sliced artichoke hearts, capers, and pitted kalamata olives. For convenience, use bottled marinara sauce.

Slow-Cooker Favorites

*T*he original heyday of the slow cooker or Crock-Pot occurred during the 1970s, when thrifty cooks used the appliance to cook tough cuts of meat. In recent years, the slow cooker has reemerged and is more popular than ever. The good news for vegan cooks is that the slow cooker can be an easy and economical way to cook bean dishes and lots of other recipes. You can save money on your electric bill as well as your food bill by making one-dish meals in your slow cooker.

Easy to assemble, these recipes are also convenient because they cook unattended while you do other things. Imagine coming home to a simmering pot of Barley Vegetable Stew (page 204), Curried Yellow Split Pea Soup (page 202), or Tempeh Pot au Feu (page 210), as well as other tempting dishes such as Tabbouleh-Stuffed Peppers (page 212) or Smoky Red Bean Chili with Chipotle-Cornbread Dumplings (page 206).

Many of these recipes, such as the Slow-Cooker Seitan Pot Roast (page 213), make enough so you can get two different meals out of them—another great way to save time and money.

Note: Other than dried beans, which can take up to twelve hours to cook in a slow cooker, many vegan recipes are ready to eat within six hours. The main reason for this is that there are no tough cuts of meat to tenderize— plant-based foods simply don't take as long to cook. If you need to be away from the house for longer than the prescribed cooking time, you might want to invest in a kitchen appliance timer (available at hardware stores) so that you can set your cooker to start cooking an hour or so after you're gone. If your cooker has a "keep warm" function, it will keep your meal hot until you get home. (For instructions on cooking dried beans, see page 46.)

So Easy Vegetable Soup

<$1.00
per serving

Makes 6 servings

You can use this versatile soup as a pattern and include whatever is on hand or in season. For example, add fresh zucchini or yellow summer squash and your favorite fresh herbs (add the fresh herbs at the end of cooking time). White or sweet potatoes are good additions, as is winter squash. Chopped leafy greens such as spinach or chard may be added during the last half hour of cooking time. Add the cooked grain or pasta near the end of cooking time, or spoon some into the bottom of each soup bowl before you ladle out the soup.

1 tablespoon olive oil	1 (14.5-ounce) can diced tomatoes, undrained
1 medium yellow onion, minced	1 teaspoon dried basil
2 garlic cloves, minced	1 teaspoon dried savory
2 medium carrots, chopped	¼ teaspoon black pepper
1 celery rib, chopped	2 tablespoons minced fresh parsley
4 ounces trimmed fresh or frozen cut green beans	5 cups vegetable stock (page 45)
1 cup frozen lima beans	Salt
1½ cups cooked or 1 (15.5-ounce) can white beans, drained and rinsed	

1. Pour the oil into a 4-quart slow cooker and turn it on Low. Add the onion, garlic, carrots, and celery and place the lid on the cooker.

2. If using fresh green beans, cut them into 1-inch pieces. Add the green beans to the cooker along with the lima beans, white beans, and tomatoes with their juice. Add the basil, savory, pepper, parsley, stock, and salt to taste. (The amount of salt needed depends on the saltiness of your stock.)

3. Place the lid back on the cooker. Cook for 6 to 8 hours or until the vegetables are tender. Taste and adjust seasonings, if necessary. Serve hot.

Variation

For added flavor (though it means an extra pot to wash), instead of placing all the ingredients directly in the slow cooker, heat the oil in a large skillet over medium heat. Add the onion, garlic, and carrots. Cover and cook until softened, about 5 minutes, then add to the cooker and proceed with the recipe.

Splurge a Little

Use fresh herbs instead of dried.

To Sauté or Not to Sauté

One of the things people like about the slow cooker is the notion that you can dump everything in the Crock-Pot, turn it on, and walk away. And in many cases you can. But it's also true that the flavor of many recipes can be improved by taking an extra 5 or 10 minutes (and an extra pot) to start the recipe on top of the stove, primarily in the form of cooking onions and garlic in a little oil before adding to the Crock-Pot. This step enriches the flavor and improves the texture of the recipes. Since opinion on this point seems divided, I've made that extra step an optional variation in some of the recipes in this chapter.

Black Bean Soup with Kale and Rice

<$1.00 per serving

Makes 4 to 6 servings

The only thing better than a pot of black bean soup is black bean soup that also contains greens and rice for a hearty one-dish meal.

1 tablespoon olive oil
1 medium yellow onion, chopped
1 medium carrot, chopped
3 garlic cloves, minced
½ cup long-grain brown rice
4 cups cooked or 3 (15.5-ounce) cans black beans, drained and rinsed
1 (14.5-ounce) can diced fire-roasted tomatoes, undrained

1 teaspoon ground cumin
1 teaspoon dried thyme
½ teaspoon smoked paprika
1 teaspoon salt
¼ teaspoon black pepper
3 cups chopped kale
5 cups vegetable stock (page 45)

1 Pour the oil into a 4-quart slow cooker and turn it on Low. Add the onion, carrot, garlic, and rice.

2 Add the beans, tomatoes with their juice, cumin, thyme, paprika, salt, and pepper. Add the kale, pour in the stock, and stir to combine. Place the lid on the slow cooker and cook until the rice is cooked and the vegetables are tender, 6 to 8 hours. Taste and adjust the seasonings, if necessary. Serve hot.

Variation

For added flavor (though it means an extra pot to wash), instead of placing all the ingredients directly in the slow cooker, heat the oil in a large skillet over medium heat. Add the onion, carrot, and garlic. Cover and cook until softened, about 5 minutes, then add to the cooker and proceed with the recipe.

Splurge a Little

Add ¼ cup dry sherry to the pot; add 1 pureed chipotle in adobo; garnish with chopped vegan pepperoni or sausage.

Moroccan-Inspired Lentil Soup

<$1.50 per serving

Makes 4 to 6 servings

Lentils are enjoyed throughout the world as a delicious and inexpensive protein source. This thick and rich soup is inspired by the fragrant flavors of Morocco. If you enjoy a little heat, accompany the soup with a small bowl of harissa sauce, a spicy Moroccan condiment, to add to taste. Optional: Add cooked chickpeas, rice, or couscous to your soup bowls, then ladle the soup on top.

1 tablespoon olive oil	1 (28-ounce) can diced tomatoes, undrained
1 medium yellow onion, chopped	
2 medium carrots, chopped	1 cup brown lentils, picked over, rinsed, and drained
1 small green bell pepper, chopped	
3 garlic cloves, minced	3 cups vegetable stock (page 45)
2 teaspoons minced fresh ginger	1 cup apple juice
1½ teaspoons ground cumin	½ cup mixed dried fruit, chopped
1½ teaspoons ground coriander	Salt and black pepper
½ teaspoon ground cinnamon	2 tablespoons minced fresh parsley
¼ teaspoon ground cayenne	1 tablespoon fresh lemon juice
¼ teaspoon turmeric	

❶ Pour the oil into a 4-quart slow cooker.

❷ Add the onion, carrots, bell pepper, garlic, and ginger. Add the cumin, coriander, cinnamon, cayenne, and turmeric, then stir in the tomatoes with their juice and lentils.

❸ Pour in the vegetable stock and apple juice, then add the dried fruit. Season with salt and pepper to taste. (The amount of salt needed will depend on the saltiness of your stock.) Place the lid on the slow cooker and turn the heat to Low. Cook until the lentils and vegetables are tender, about 8 hours. When ready to serve, stir in the parsley and lemon juice. Taste and adjust seasonings, if necessary. Serve hot.

Curried Yellow Split Pea Soup

<$1.00 per serving

Makes 4 to 6 servings

This thick and flavorful soup is very much like an Indian dal and a great way to enjoy split peas. I use yellow peas to enhance the golden color of the curry powder. As an addition, you could stir in some chopped fresh spinach or chard during the last few minutes of cooking time. For even more substance, serve in shallow bowls over cooked rice.

1 tablespoon canola or other neutral oil

1 medium yellow onion, chopped

1 medium carrot, chopped

1 pound yellow split peas, picked over, rinsed, and drained

1 tablespoon hot or mild curry powder

1 teaspoon ground coriander

½ teaspoon ground cumin

¼ teaspoon ground cayenne

6 cups vegetable stock (page 45)

Salt and black pepper

Minced fresh cilantro or parsley

1. Pour the oil into a 4-quart slow cooker. Add the onion, carrot, peas, curry powder, coriander, cumin, and cayenne. Stir in the stock and season with salt and pepper to taste. (The amount of salt needed will depend on the saltiness of your stock.)

2. Put the lid on the cooker and turn the heat to Low. Cook until the peas are tender, stirring once if possible, about 8 hours. Stir in the cilantro. Taste and adjust the seasonings, if necessary. Serve hot garnished with cilantro.

Splurge a Little

Garnish with vegan yogurt.

Three Spicy Sisters Stew

<$1.50 per serving

Makes 4 to 6 servings

If you've heard the Iroquois legend of the Three Sisters, then you know that they considered corn, beans, and squash inseparable "sisters" that needed to be grown together in the same mounds to maximize their growth and sustainability. Not only do these charming sisters grow well together, but they are also complementary when cooked together in recipes such as this delicious stew. If you prefer the sisters without the spice, omit the chiles and cayenne.

1 tablespoon olive oil
1 medium yellow onion, chopped
1 medium green or red bell pepper, chopped
2 garlic cloves, minced
1 teaspoon ground cumin
1 teaspoon ground coriander
½ teaspoon dried marjoram
1½ pounds butternut squash, peeled, halved, seeded, and cut into ½-inch chunks
½ teaspoon salt

¼ teaspoon ground cayenne
1 (14.5-ounce) can diced tomatoes, undrained
1 or 2 chipotle chiles in adobo, minced
3 cups cooked or 2 (15.5-ounce) cans pinto beans, drained and rinsed
1 cup vegetable stock (page 45)
2 cups thawed frozen corn
2 tablespoons minced fresh parsley or cilantro

❶ Pour the oil into a 4- to 5-quart slow cooker and turn it on Low. Add the onion, bell pepper, garlic, cumin, coriander, and marjoram. Put the lid on while you assemble the rest of the ingredients.

❷ Add the squash, salt, cayenne, tomatoes with their juice, chipotle chiles, beans, and stock. Put the lid back on the slow cooker and cook until the vegetables are tender, about 8 hours.

❸ About 15 minutes before serving time, stir in the corn and parsley. Taste and adjust the seasonings, if necessary. Serve hot.

Barley Vegetable Stew

<$1.00
per serving

Makes 6 servings

Barley is an inexpensive and delicious grain that is especially good in stews, soups, and salads. It takes well to the slow cooker, too, as evidenced in this hearty and comforting stew made with white beans, potatoes, and mushrooms and seasoned with dill and thyme.

1 tablespoon olive oil

1 medium yellow onion, chopped

2 medium carrots, thinly sliced

1 celery rib, sliced

3 garlic cloves, minced

1 pound red-skinned potatoes, cut into ½-inch dice

1½ cups sliced white mushrooms

¾ cup pearl barley

1 (14.5-ounce) can diced tomatoes, undrained

2 tablespoon tomato paste (optional)

1½ cups cooked or 1 (15.5-ounce) can white beans, drained and rinsed

2 teaspoons fresh minced dill weed or 1 teaspoon dried

1 teaspoon dried thyme

½ teaspoon paprika

2 cups vegetable stock (page 45)

½ cup dry white wine

1 large bay leaf

½ teaspoon salt

¼ teaspoon black pepper

1 Pour the oil into a 4-quart slow cooker. Add the onion, carrots, celery, garlic, potatoes, mushrooms, and barley. Stir in the tomatoes with their juice, tomato paste, if using, white beans, dill weed, thyme, paprika, stock, and wine. Add the bay leaf, salt, and pepper. (The amount of salt needed will depend on the saltiness of your stock.)

2 Put the lid on the slow cooker and cook on Low until the vegetables and barley are tender, about 8 hours. Remove and discard the bay leaf before serving. Serve hot.

Variation

For added flavor (though it means an extra pot to wash), instead of placing all the ingredients directly in the slow cooker, heat the oil in a large skillet over medium heat. Add the onion, carrots, and garlic. Cover and cook until softened, about 5 minutes, then add to the cooker and proceed with the recipe.

Positively Pantry Chili

Makes 4 to 6 servings

When there's no time to cook, go to the supermarket, or stand around and watch a pot, you'll be glad you have a well-stocked pantry and a slow cooker. In less than five minutes you can combine these pantry in-gredients in the cooker, then walk away. In a few hours, a hot and hearty chili will be ready to serve.

1 (24-ounce) jar chunky tomato salsa or picante sauce

¼ cup barbecue sauce or ketchup

2 tablespoons chili powder

¾ teaspoon salt

1½ teaspoons ground cumin

1 teaspoon dried oregano

½ teaspoon paprika

½ teaspoon sugar

1 cup water, or more

1½ cups cooked or 1 (15.5-ounce) can dark red kidney beans, drained and rinsed

1½ cups cooked or 1 (15.5-ounce) can black beans, drained and rinsed

1½ cups cooked or 1 (15.5-ounce) can pinto beans, drained and rinsed

½ cup bulgur (optional)

1 (16-ounce) can corn kernels, drained or 2 cups thawed frozen corn kernels

❶ Pour the salsa and barbecue sauce into a 4- to 5-quart slow cooker. Add the chili powder, salt, cumin, oregano, paprika, and sugar, and stir to blend. Stir in 1 cup of water, then add all the beans and bulgur, if using. (If using bulgur, add an additional 1 cup water.) Mix well.

❷ Cover and cook on Low until the chili is thick and the flavors are well combined, about 6 hours. About 10 minutes before you're ready to serve, stir in the corn and then taste and adjust the seasonings, if necessary. Serve hot.

Variation

Stovetop Version: For a quicker version of this chili, combine all the ingredients in a pot and simmer on the stove for 45 minutes to an hour, stirring occasionally.

Splurge a Little

Garnish with diced avocado.

Smoky Red Bean Chili with Chipotle-Cornbread Dumplings

<$1.50 per serving

Makes 4 to 6 servings

Making chili in a slow cooker deepens its flavor, in this case the sultry intensity of smoked paprika and chipotle chiles. The rich chipotle-flecked cornbread dumplings on top make it hard to resist. To vary the texture, substitute 1½ cups chopped seitan for part of the beans. Freeze any remaining chipotles for another use.

Chili

1 tablespoon olive oil

1 large red onion, minced

1 medium green bell pepper, minced

2 garlic cloves, minced

2 tablespoons chili powder

1 teaspoon smoked paprika

1½ teaspoons ground cumin

½ teaspoon dried oregano

1 (14.5-ounce) can crushed tomatoes

1 (14.5-ounce) can diced tomatoes, undrained

4 cups cooked or 3 (15.5-ounce) cans dark red kidney beans, drained and rinsed

1 chipotle chile in adobo, minced

1 cup water

1 teaspoon salt

¼ teaspoon black pepper

Dumplings

1 cup yellow cornmeal

½ cup all-purpose flour

1½ teaspoons baking powder

¼ teaspoon salt

¾ cup plain unsweetened soy milk

2 tablespoons olive oil

1 or 2 chipotle chiles in adobo, finely minced

❶ **Make the chili:** Pour the oil into a 4- to 5-quart slow cooker. Add the onion, bell pepper, and garlic.

❷ Add the chili powder, paprika, cumin, and oregano. Stir in the crushed tomatoes, diced tomatoes with their juice, beans, chipotle, water, salt, and black pepper. Put the lid on and turn the heat to Low. Cook until the chili is thick and the flavors have developed, 6 to 8 hours.

③ About 45 minutes before serving time, make the dumplings: In a medium bowl, combine the cornmeal, flour, baking powder, and salt. Stir in the soy milk, oil, and chipotle until just combined. Do not overmix.

④ Increase the heat to High and drop the batter by the spoonful onto the hot chili. Cover and cook on High until the dumplings are cooked through, about 30 minutes. Serve immediately.

Splurge a Little

Replace the green bell pepper with a red bell pepper.

About the Beans in These Recipes

Other than the recipes that use lentils and split peas, recipes calling for beans use cooked beans. The reason for this is threefold: (1) Beans cooked in a slow cooker should be prepared separately because they take longer to cook than other ingredients, and this will also allow you to cook a large amount of beans that can be portioned and frozen for use in recipes; (2) cooking the beans separately before adding to the recipe improves their digestibility; (3) by using cooked beans in the recipes, this allows you to use canned or other "on hand" beans for quick assembly.

If you want to cook dried beans in a slow cooker, follow the instructions given on page 46.

Seitan and Mushroom Goulash

<$2.00 per serving>

Makes 4 to 6 servings

Hungarian goulash is a hearty stew traditionally made with beef and sauerkraut, made creamy with the addition of sour cream. In this version I use seitan and mushrooms, which have a natural affinity to sauerkraut. Vegan sour cream adds a luscious creamy texture to the sauce. Serve over cooked egg-free noodles. If egg-free vegan noodles are unavailable, fettuccine noodles broken into thirds are a good alternative.

1 tablespoon olive oil

1 medium yellow onion, finely chopped

8 ounces seitan (page 50), cut into ½-inch dice

8 ounces white mushrooms, lightly rinsed, patted dry, and halved, quartered, or thickly sliced

2 cups sauerkraut, drained and rinsed

1 (14.5-ounce) can diced tomatoes, undrained

1 tablespoon sweet Hungarian paprika

¼ cup dry white wine

1 teaspoon caraway seeds

2 tablespoons tomato paste

¾ cup vegetable stock (page 45)

Salt and black pepper

½ cup **Vegan Sour Cream** (page 42)

Cooked hot noodles

1 Pour the oil into the bottom of a 4-quart slow cooker and turn it on High. Cover with the lid while you assemble the remaining ingredients.

2 Add the onion, seitan, mushrooms, sauerkraut, tomatoes, paprika, wine, and caraway seeds.

3 In a small bowl, combine the tomato paste and about ½ cup of the stock, stirring to blend. Add the tomato paste mixture to the slow cooker, along with the remaining stock. Season with salt and pepper to taste. (The amount of salt needed will depend on the saltiness of your stock.) Put the lid on the slow cooker and turn the heat down to Low. Cook until the vegetables are tender and the flavors have blended, 6 to 8 hours.

4 Just before serving, stir the sour cream into the goulash. Taste and adjust seasonings, if necessary. Serve hot over noodles.

Four-Grain "Polenta"

Makes 6 servings

Loaded with protein from tofu, chickpeas, and four different grains, this flavorful and economical comfort food dish reminds me of a cross between polenta and stuffing—and it can be served like either one. To serve it like stuffing, spoon it onto your plates and top with Creamy Mushroom Gravy (page 31). For a polenta-like dish, replace the thyme and sage with basil. Then, to serve, spoon it into shallow bowls and top with Marinara Sauce (page 32). It's also good topped with sautéed mushrooms or garlicky greens, roasted diced vegetables, or Smoky Tempeh Bits (page 58).

1 tablespoon olive oil	$\frac{1}{3}$ cup millet
1 large yellow onion, chopped	$\frac{1}{4}$ cup minced fresh parsley
2 celery ribs, minced	1 teaspoon dried sage
1 medium carrot, minced	1 teaspoon dried thyme
1 pound extra-firm tofu, drained and crumbled	1 teaspoon dried marjoram
	$\frac{1}{2}$ teaspoon salt
1½ cups cooked or 1 (15.5-ounce) can chickpeas, drained and rinsed	$\frac{1}{4}$ teaspoon black pepper
	$\frac{1}{3}$ cup old-fashioned oats
	$\frac{1}{3}$ cup yellow cornmeal
$\frac{1}{4}$ cup soy sauce	2½ cups vegetable stock
$\frac{1}{3}$ cup brown rice	(page 45)

1 Lightly oil the insert of a 4-quart slow cooker. Pour the oil into the slow cooker. Add the onion, celery, and carrot. Put the lid on the cooker and turn to High while you assemble the rest of the ingredients.

2 In a food processor, combine the tofu, chickpeas, and soy sauce, and process until smooth. Set aside.

3 Add the remaining ingredients to the slow cooker.

4 Stir in the tofu-chickpea mixture and mix well to combine. Put the lid back on the slow cooker and turn down to Low. Cook until the grains are tender and the liquid is absorbed, 6 to 8 hours. Serve hot.

Splurge a Little

Drizzle with balsamic syrup or walnut oil.

Tempeh Pot au Feu

Makes 4 servings

Did you ever notice how almost anything French sounds delicious and expensive? This *pot au feu* (literally "pot on fire") is delicious but only sounds expensive—it's a country French mélange of super-cheap veggies and tempeh simmered in a tasty broth. This makes a great Sunday dinner and depending on the size of your cooker, you can add more veggies to feed a crowd or, if you have a smaller slow cooker, cut back on the volume of ingredients. Serve with a dab of horseradish or mustard on the side and sliced and toasted baguettes to sop up the flavorful broth.

1 tablespoon olive oil

8 ounces tempeh, cut into 1-inch strips

1 medium yellow onion, diced

3 small white potatoes, halved or quartered

2 medium carrots, cut into matchsticks

2 small turnips, peeled and quartered

1 small rutabaga, peeled and cut into ½-inch slices

2 celery ribs, halved lengthwise and cut into 2-inch pieces

4 garlic cloves, crushed

1 bouquet garni (see Note)

4 green onions, ends trimmed and cut into 2-inch pieces

4 cups vegetable stock (page 45)

½ cup dry white wine

1 teaspoon dried thyme

2 tablespoons chopped fresh parsley

1 teaspoon salt

¼ teaspoon black pepper

Coarse-ground brown mustard, for garnish

Horseradish, for garnish

1 In a large skillet, heat the oil over medium heat. Add the tempeh and cook until golden brown, about 10 minutes. Transfer the tempeh to a 6- to 7-quart slow cooker.

2 Add the onion, potatoes, carrots, turnips, rutabaga, celery, and garlic to the cooker. Add the bouquet garni and the green onions. Add the stock, wine, thyme, parsley, salt, and pepper. (The amount of salt needed will depend on the saltiness of your stock.) Cover and cook on Low until the vegetables are tender, 7 to 8 hours.

③ Remove the bouquet garni and discard. Transfer the vegetables and tempeh to a large platter. Pour the broth into small cups and serve as a first course or alongside the entrée. Accompany with small bowls of the mustard and horseradish.

Variation

Use sliced seitan instead of the tempeh. Add a small head of cabbage, cut into wedges.

Note: *For the bouquet garni:* In a 5-inch square of cheesecloth (use a coffee filter or tea ball if you don't have cheesecloth), place the following: 1 teaspoon whole cloves, 1 teaspoon peppercorns, 2 or 3 crumbled bay leaves, 1 teaspoon celery seeds, and 1 teaspoon dried thyme. Close up the cheesecloth and tie with kitchen twine.

Splurge a Little

If desired, include leeks and parsnips in the vegetable mélange, omitting the green onions and using fewer turnips or carrots. Serve with cornichons on the side.

Tabbouleh-Stuffed Peppers

Makes 4 servings

The slow cooker is an ideal way to cook stuffed peppers, and the fragrance in the house while they're cooking is wonderful. After about 6 hours, the peppers may start to get too soft and lose their shape, so this recipe should be made on a day when you'll be around to check on them within that time frame.

2 cups water

Salt

1 cup bulgur

1½ cups cooked or 1 (15.5-ounce) can chickpeas, rinsed and drained

1 cup chopped fresh parsley

½ cup chopped green onions

2 garlic cloves, finely minced

3 tablespoons olive oil

3 tablespoons fresh lemon juice

¼ teaspoon ground cayenne

4 large green bell peppers

1 (28-ounce) can diced tomatoes, undrained

1 teaspoon sugar

½ teaspoon dried oregano

½ teaspoon ground cumin

Black pepper

❶ In a large saucepan, bring the water to boil over high heat. Salt the water and stir in the bulgur. Cover, remove from heat, and set aside until all liquid is absorbed, about 5 minutes. Stir in the chickpeas, parsley, green onions, garlic, oil, lemon juice, cayenne, and salt to taste. Mix well, then taste and adjust the seasonings, if necessary.

❷ Slice off the tops of the bell peppers and remove the seeds and membranes. Arrange the peppers upright in a 6-quart slow cooker.

❸ Spoon the bulgur mixture into the pepper cavities, packing well.

❹ In a medium bowl, combine the diced tomatoes with their juice, sugar, oregano, cumin, and salt and black pepper to taste. Mix well, then pour the tomato mixture around the peppers in the slow cooker.

❺ Cover and cook on Low until the peppers are tender but still hold their shape, about 6 hours. Serve hot.

Slow-Cooker Seitan Pot Roast

<$1.00 per serving

Makes 4 to 6 servings

This pot roast makes regular appearances on our dinner menu and rewards us with enough leftovers for a different meal on another night.

1 medium yellow onion, coarsely chopped

1¾ cups wheat gluten flour (vital wheat gluten)

¼ cup nutritional yeast

1 teaspoon onion powder

1 teaspoon dried thyme

Salt and black pepper

1½ cups water

3 tablespoons soy sauce

1 tablespoon ketchup or tomato sauce

1 pound carrots, cut into ¼-inch slices

1 pound small red-skinned potatoes, halved or quartered

1 cup vegetable stock (page 45)

2 garlic cloves, crushed

❶ Lightly oil the insert of a 6- to 7-quart slow cooker and spread the onion evenly in the bottom.

❷ In a large bowl, combine the flour, yeast, onion powder, ½ teaspoon of the thyme, ½ teaspoon of salt, and ¼ teaspoon of pepper. Add the water, soy sauce, and ketchup. Mix well, adding a little more water if the mixture is too dry, then knead for 2 minutes, until smooth. Shape the gluten to fit inside your cooker and place it on top of the onions.

❸ Arrange the carrots and potatoes in the cooker around the seitan. Season the vegetables with salt and pepper to taste, and add the stock, garlic, and the remaining ½ teaspoon of the thyme. Put the lid on the slow cooker and cook on Low until the seitan and vegetables are cooked, about 8 hours.

❹ To serve, remove the vegetables and seitan from the slow cooker. Cut the seitan into slices and arrange them on a serving platter. Surround with the vegetables and spoon the cooking liquid over all. Serve hot.

Note: This recipe is best made in a 6- to 7-quart oval slow cooker. If you have a smaller 4-quart slow cooker, you can still make the pot roast, but in order to not overfill the pot, use only about half as many vegetables or cook your vegetables another way, either in the oven or on top of the stove.

Corned Seitan and Cabbage

<$1.00 per serving

Makes 4 to 6 servings

Whether you want to celebrate St. Patrick's Day in style or are simply looking for the main ingredient to make a fantastic vegan Reuben sandwich, this corned seitan recipe won't let you down. Look for pickling spices in the spice aisle in your supermarket.

1 medium yellow onion, coarsely chopped

2 garlic cloves, crushed

1 small head cabbage, sliced, reserving 2 large leaves

Salt and black pepper

2 cups wheat gluten flour (vital wheat gluten)

1 teaspoon onion powder

1 teaspoon ground coriander

½ teaspoon ground allspice

1½ cups water, or more as needed

3 tablespoons soy sauce

3 tablespoons plus 1 teaspoon coarse brown mustard

1 teaspoon apple cider vinegar

3 tablespoons light brown sugar

2 teaspoons pickling spices

1 pound Yukon Gold potatoes

1 cup vegetable stock (page 45)

1 Lightly oil the insert of a 6- to 7-quart slow cooker. Arrange the onion, garlic, and sliced cabbage in the bottom of the slow cooker. Season with salt and pepper to taste.

2 In a large bowl, combine the flour, onion powder, coriander, allspice, ½ teaspoon of salt, and ¼ teaspoon of pepper. Add the water, soy sauce, 1 teaspoon of the mustard, and vinegar. Mix well, adding a little more water if the mixture is too dry, then knead for 2 minutes, until smooth. Shape the seitan to fit inside your cooker.

3 In a small bowl, combine the remaining 3 tablespoons mustard and the sugar until well blended, then spread evenly on top of the seitan. Sprinkle the pickling spices on top, pressing them with your hand to embed them in the mustard mixture.

4 Carefully place the seitan in the cooker on top of the two cabbage leaves. Cut the potatoes into chunks and arrange them around the seitan. Pour the stock over the potatoes and season them with salt and pepper. Put the lid on the slow cooker and cook on Low until the seitan and vegetables are cooked, about 8 hours.

⑤ To serve, remove the vegetables and seitan from the slow cooker. Cut the seitan into slices and arrange them on a serving platter. Surround with the vegetables and spoon the cooking liquid over all. Serve hot.

Note: As with the pot roast recipe on page 213, this is best when made in a larger cooker to accommodate vegetables, but if you have a smaller 4-quart slow cooker, you can still make this recipe—just use half the amount of vegetables so you do not overfill the cooker. Alternately, you can cook the potatoes and cabbage in the oven or on top of the stove and just use the slow cooker to cook the seitan on top of the onion and cabbage leaves (these give added flavor to the seitan and help hold its shape), adding the vegetable stock and garlic.

Sweet Delights

*L*et's face it, to most of us, dessert can be considered a splurge of one kind or another, whether it be calories, time, or money—or all three.

The focus of the recipes in this chapter is to provide delicious and wholesome desserts that economize on those elements but don't taste like it. You won't find expensive or time-consuming recipes here. Instead, look for the old-fashioned homey goodness of cobblers, crisps, cookies, and puddings. I've also included intriguing variations on brownies and tiramisù as well as an irresistible apple clafouti and a moist and delicious Italian polenta cake.

Perhaps most importantly, many of the recipes are made with on-hand pantry ingredients and seasonal fruit so that you can whip up a tasty dessert at a moment's notice.

Gold Bar Cookies

Makes 24 cookies

While you can't take these gold bars to the bank, these bar cookies do provide dividends: They're easy to make with pantry ingredients and the recipe makes a lot. Best of all, they're versatile. When my mother used to make them as an after-school treat, she'd change up the toppings according to what she had in the house.

1¾ cup quick-cooking oats
1 cup all-purpose flour
1 cup light brown sugar
1 teaspoon baking powder
1 teaspoon ground cinnamon
1 teaspoon salt
½ cup vegan margarine, softened

¼ cup creamy peanut butter, softened
1 (8-ounce) jar peach or apricot preserves
½ cup golden raisins
½ cup ground unsalted roasted peanuts

❶ Preheat the oven to 375°F. Grease a 9 × 13-inch baking pan and set aside.

❷ In a food processor, combine the oats, flour, sugar, baking powder, cinnamon, and salt. Pulse to mix well. Add the margarine and peanut butter and pulse until crumbly.

❸ Place about 3 cups of the crumb mixture into the bottom of the prepared pan and press it evenly with your hands to form the cookie base. Reserve the remaining mixture.

❹ Place the preserves in a small bowl and stir until smooth. Spread over the top of the cookie base to within ¼ inch of the edge.

❺ Add the raisins and peanuts to the remaining crumb mixture and sprinkle it over the top, pressing it into the fruit.

❻ Bake until golden, 25 to 30 minutes. Set aside to cool for 15 minutes before cutting.

Variations

Use different flavored fruit spreads and add some chopped fresh or canned fruit; omit the peanuts and peanut butter entirely, or use a different nut; add vegan chocolate chips or shredded coconut to the topping mixture.

Splurge a Little

Substitute almond butter and almonds for the peanut butter and peanuts. Splurge even more by substituting pistachios or macadamias.

Cookie Cache

Fresh-baked cookies taste great and are often less expensive than other desserts. Here are two ways to make sure you always have a cache of cookies on hand.

1. **Freeze some dough.** Instead of baking an entire batch of cookies at once, wrap some of the cookie dough and stash it in the freezer to bake another time—even if it's just a few days later. (Cookies fresh from the oven taste better than three-day-old cookies.)

2. **Freeze some cookies.** If you find yourself with more baked cookies than you can easily eat in a day or two, wrap up some of them and freeze them. Then just thaw at room temperature next time you need something sweet.

Sesame Shortbread Cookies

Makes about 3 dozen cookies

These rich-tasting cookies are imbued with the flavor of sesame, tahini in the dough and toasted sesame seeds on the outside, after a quick dip in chocolate.

¾ cup vegan margarine, softened

¼ cup tahini (sesame paste), softened

¾ cup packed light brown sugar

2 teaspoons pure vanilla extract

2 cups all-purpose flour

½ cup vegan semisweet chocolate chips

½ cup toasted sesame seeds (page 14)

❶ Preheat the oven to 325°F. In a large bowl, combine the margarine, tahini, and sugar. Cream together until smooth. Beat in the vanilla, then add the flour, one-third at a time, until it is all incorporated.

❷ Divide the dough into quarters and shape each portion into a ½-inch-thick log. Cut the logs into 2-inch pieces and arrange them on ungreased baking sheets, about 1½ inches apart. Bake until lightly browned, 15 to 17 minutes. Let cool on wire racks.

❸ Melt the chocolate in a saucepan over low heat or in a microwave-safe bowl in the microwave for about 1 minute. Stir until smooth and set aside. Place the sesame seeds in a shallow bowl. Set aside.

❹ Dip one end of each cookie into the melted chocolate, then into the sesame seeds. Place the dipped cookies on waxed paper and refrigerate to firm up chocolate before serving, about 30 minutes. Refrigerate unused cookies in a container with a tight-fitting lid. These cookies taste best when eaten on the same day they are made but keep well for up to 3 days.

Variation

Peanutty Shortbread Cookies: For an even more economical version, substitute peanut butter for the tahini and ground or crushed unsalted roasted peanuts for the sesame seeds.

Chocolate Oatmeal–Peanut Butter Cookies

Makes about 24 cookies

Now three favorite cookie flavors—chocolate, oatmeal, and peanut but-ter—are combined in one easy cookie. Because these yummy cookies are no-bake, they save the cost of firing up the oven. And since they're made with economical pantry ingredients, they're also kinder to the budget than bakery cookies.

⅓ cup vegan margarine

1 cup sugar

⅓ cup plain unsweetened or vanilla soy milk

¾ cup creamy peanut butter

1 teaspoon pure vanilla extract

Pinch salt

2 cups quick-cooking oats

¾ cup vegan semisweet chocolate chips

❶ In a medium saucepan, melt the margarine over medium heat. Stir in the sugar and soy milk. Cook, stirring until it just comes to a boil. Cook, stir-ring, for 1 to 2 minutes to dissolve the sugar.

❷ Remove the saucepan from the heat. Add the peanut butter, vanilla, and salt, stirring until well blended. Add the oats and chocolate chips and stir until well mixed.

❸ Drop heaping tablespoons of the cookie mixture onto a baking sheet. Set aside at room temperature until firm, about 30 minutes.

Chocolate Cupcakes with Peanut Butter Frosting

Makes 12 cupcakes

When you love both chocolate and peanut butter, it doesn't get much better than these deliciously decadent cupcakes, an indulgent treat for children and adults made with on-hand ingredients.

Cupcakes
1²⁄₃ cups all-purpose flour
½ cup unsweetened cocoa powder
½ teaspoon baking powder
½ teaspoon baking soda
½ teaspoon salt
1¼ cups granulated sugar
½ cup vegan margarine, softened
1 cup warm water
1 teaspoon pure vanilla extract

Frosting
1 cup creamy peanut butter
½ cup vegan margarine, softened
1 teaspoon pure vanilla extract
½ cup confectioners' sugar

❶ **Make the cupcakes:** Preheat the oven to 350°F. Grease or line a 12-cup muffin tin with paper liners. Set aside.

❷ In a large bowl, combine the flour, cocoa, baking powder, baking soda, and salt. Set aside.

❸ In a separate large bowl, cream together the sugar and margarine. Add the water and vanilla and mix until smooth. Add the flour mixture, a little at a time, and mix until well incorporated. Beat until smooth, 1 minute more.

❹ Spoon the batter into the prepared tin, filling the cups about two-thirds full. Bake until a toothpick inserted in the center of a cupcake comes out clean, about 25 minutes. Set aside to cool on a wire rack for about 20 minutes or until completely cool.

❺ **Make the frosting:** In a food processor, blend the peanut butter, margarine, and vanilla until smooth. Add the sugar and process until smooth and creamy. Scrape into a medium bowl and set aside.

6 When the cupcakes are completely cool, frost them with the frosting. These taste best if eaten on the same day that they are made. If not using right away, cover and store at room temperature for up to 2 days.

Splurge a Little

Substitute almond butter for the peanut butter in the frosting.

Italian Polenta Cake

<50¢
per serving

Makes 8 servings

Polenta, the darling of Italian *povero* cooking, shows its versatility in this delicious, moist cake. Many versions of this lovely golden cake exist throughout Italy; some include almonds, others use grated orange zest or raisins. This version includes all three, but the raisins are optional.

1½ cups all-purpose flour
½ cup polenta or yellow cornmeal
½ cup finely ground almonds
2 teaspoons baking powder
½ teaspoon salt
1 cup sugar
¼ cup vegan margarine, softened
¼ cup olive oil

1 teaspoon pure vanilla extract
½ teaspoon almond extract
   (optional)
2 teaspoons grated orange zest
1 cup plain unsweetened or vanilla
   soy milk
1 cup golden raisins (optional)

1 Preheat the oven to 350°F. Lightly grease a 9-inch springform pan and set aside. In a medium bowl, combine the flour, cornmeal, almonds, baking powder, and salt.

2 In a separate medium bowl, combine the sugar, margarine, oil, vanilla, and almond extract, if using. Cream together until smooth. Add the orange zest and mix until blended. Stir in the soy milk a little at a time until incorporated. Stir in the flour mixture, mixing until just blended. Stir in the raisins, if using.

3 Use the rubber spatula to scrape the batter evenly into the prepared pan. Bake until the cake springs back when lightly pressed and a toothpick comes out clean, about 40 minutes.

4 Let the cake cool on a rack for 15 to 20 minutes before carefully removing the sides of the pan. Cool another 20 to 30 minutes longer before slicing. Serve at room temperature.

Splurge a Little
Brush the top of the cake with some warmed, strained orange marmalade and sprinkle toasted pine nuts around the perimeter of the top.

Chocolate Surprise Brownies

<50¢ per serving

Makes 16 brownies

I like the idea of using inexpensive and healthy ingredients in dessert recipes, so I was intrigued by the numerous brownie recipes floating around on the internet that call for black beans. After experimenting a bit, I've come up with my own version that contains not only black beans but other surprises including coffee and fruit. Perhaps the biggest surprise of all is that these rich, chocolatey brownies have a wonderful flavor and are easy to make.

1 cup cooked or canned black beans, drained and rinsed

½ cup sugar

3 tablespoons canola or other neutral oil

4 tablespoons unsweetened cocoa powder

1 ripe banana

2 tablespoons instant coffee

2 teaspoons pure vanilla extract

½ cup all-purpose flour

2 teaspoons baking powder

⅛ teaspoon salt

¾ cup vegan semisweet chocolate chips

½ cup walnut pieces (optional)

1 Preheat the oven to 350°F. Grease an 8-inch square baking pan and set aside.

2 In a blender or food processor, combine the black beans, sugar, and oil, and blend until smooth. Add the banana, coffee, and vanilla, and blend until smooth.

3 Scrape the mixture into a large mixing bowl. Add the flour, baking powder, and salt and mix until smooth. Stir in the chocolate chips and walnut pieces, if using.

4 Scrape the batter into the prepared pan. Bake until a toothpick inserted in the center comes out clean, 25 to 30 minutes. Let cool completely in the pan on a wire rack, then refrigerate for several hours before cutting into squares.

Pumpkin Spice Cake with Chocolate Glaze

Makes 12 servings

This moist and delicious cake is great anytime, but will be especially welcome during the fall and winter months when you need to serve a crowd. For a beautiful presentation (and easier serving), use a Bundt pan for this recipe. If you don't have a Bundt pan, you can bake it in a 9 × 13-inch baking pan. The cake can be made without the glaze or with a different icing if you prefer.

Cake
½ cup plain unsweetened or vanilla
    soy milk
2 teaspoons apple cider vinegar
½ cup vegan margarine, softened
1 cup light brown sugar
1 (15-ounce) can solid-pack
    pumpkin
1 teaspoon pure vanilla extract
2 cups all-purpose flour
2 teaspoons baking powder
1 teaspoon baking soda
½ teaspoon salt
1½ teaspoons ground cinnamon
½ teaspoon ground allspice
½ teaspoon ground ginger
½ teaspoon ground nutmeg

Chocolate Glaze
¾ cup vegan semisweet
    chocolate chips
2 tablespoons vegan margarine
1 cup confectioners' sugar
1 to 2 tablespoons plain
    unsweetened or vanilla soy milk

❶ **Make the cake:** Preheat the oven to 350°F. Grease a Bundt pan and set it aside.

❷ In a small bowl, combine the soy milk and vinegar and set aside. In a large bowl, cream together the margarine and sugar until light and fluffy, 2 to 3 minutes. Add the pumpkin and vanilla and beat until incorporated. Stir in the soy milk mixture and blend until smooth.

3 In a medium bowl, whisk together the flour, baking powder, baking soda, salt, and spices. Add the flour mixture to the pumpkin batter about one-third at a time, incorporating after each addition. Scrape the batter into the prepared pan and bake for about 30 minutes, or until a toothpick inserted in the center comes out clean.

4 Cool for 10 minutes in the pan on a wire rack and then invert and remove the cake from the pan. Cool completely on the wire rack.

5 **Make the glaze:** In a medium saucepan, melt the chocolate and margarine over low heat and cook, stirring, until melted.

6 Remove from heat and beat in the sugar. Gradually add the soy milk until the glaze is pourable. When the cake is completely cool, pour on the glaze.

Great Northern Apple Cake

Makes 8 servings

The secret ingredient in this moist and delicious cake is Great Northern white beans. Made with other healthy ingredients, including oats, walnuts, and, of course, apples, this is a nutritious cake to serve the kids when they want a snack—no need to tell them it's good for them!

½ cup chopped toasted walnuts

1 tablespoon vegan margarine

2 Granny Smith or other crisp apples, peeled, cored, and cut into ½-inch slices

1¼ cups light brown sugar

2 teaspoons fresh lemon juice

½ cup old-fashioned oats

1 cup cooked or canned Great Northern beans, rinsed and drained

2 tablespoons canola or other neutral oil

1 teaspoon pure vanilla extract

1 cup all-purpose flour

2 teaspoons baking powder

1½ teaspoons ground cinnamon

½ teaspoon ground allspice

1 Preheat the oven to 350°F. Lightly oil a 9-inch cake pan, sprinkle with ¼ cup of the walnuts, and set aside.

2 In a medium skillet, melt the margarine over medium heat. Add the apples, ½ cup of the sugar, and the lemon juice and cook, stirring to soften the apples and dissolve the sugar, for 3 to 4 minutes. Remove the apple slices from the pan and set aside to cool. Reserve the liquid in the pan.

3 When the apple slices are cool enough to handle, arrange them concentrically on top of the walnuts in the bottom of the prepared pan. Sprinkle the remaining ¼ cup walnuts onto the apples and set aside.

4 In a food processor, grind the oats to a fine powder. Remove the powdered oats from the food processor and set aside.

5 Add the beans, oil, and vanilla to the food processor. Add ½ cup reserved cooking liquid from the apples (if you don't have enough, add apple juice or water to equal ½ cup). Blend until smooth. Add the powdered oats, all-purpose flour, remaining ¾ cup sugar, baking powder, cinnamon, and allspice and process until well blended.

6 Scrape the batter into the prepared pan on top of the apple slices. Bake until golden brown, about 35 minutes.

7 Let cool on a wire rack for 30 minutes, then run a knife around the sides of the cake. Place a plate on top of the cake and invert. Carefully remove the pan to reveal the apple slices as the top of the cake.

Splurge a Little

Substitute ripe mangoes for the apples and pistachios or macadamias for the walnuts.

Apple Clafouti

< 50¢
per serving

Makes 8 servings

Inspired by the traditional country French dessert, this version uses applesauce in the batter and chopped sautéed apples in the base. The result is a moist and delicious dessert that is part pie and part cake. You can substitute another fruit for the apples if you wish, including pears or peaches.

3 large Granny Smith or other
  baking apples
1 tablespoon vegan margarine
½ cup plus 1 tablespoon granulated
  sugar
1½ teaspoons ground cinnamon
1 cup applesauce
¾ cup plain unsweetened or vanilla
  soy milk

2 tablespoons pure maple syrup
1 teaspoon pure vanilla extract
Pinch salt
1 cup all-purpose flour
2 teaspoons baking powder
2 tablespoons confectioners'
  sugar

❶ Preheat the oven to 375°F. Grease a 10-inch quiche dish or pie plate and set aside. Peel and core the apples and cut them into ½-inch slices.

❷ In a large skillet, melt the margarine over medium heat. Add the apples, 1 tablespoon of the sugar, and 1 teaspoon of cinnamon and cook, stirring, until the apples are softened, 3 to 4 minutes. Spread the apple slices evenly in the bottom of the prepared dish and set aside.

❸ In a large bowl, beat together the applesauce, soy milk, remaining ½ cup sugar, maple syrup, vanilla, remaining ½ teaspoon of cinnamon, and salt until smooth. Beat in the flour and baking powder until combined and smooth. Do not overmix.

❹ Pour the batter over the apples and bake until set, about 35 minutes. Cool on a wire rack for 30 minutes. Just before serving, sprinkle with confectioners' sugar. Serve warm.

Fresh Pear Galette

< 50¢
per serving

Makes 8 servings

A galette is a rustic, free-form single-crust pie. Keep this sophisticated and delicious dessert in mind when you have some ripe pears on hand or some pie dough stashed in the freezer. Although pears are used in this recipe, you can substitute another fresh fruit such as apples, peaches, or plums.

½ recipe Double Pie Crust (page 59)

¼ cup plus 2 tablespoons apricot preserves

4 to 5 ripe Bartlett pears, peeled, cored, and cut into ¼-inch slices

1 tablespoon fresh lemon juice

⅓ cup golden raisins (optional)

⅓ cup light brown sugar

½ teaspoon ground cinnamon

⅛ teaspoon ground nutmeg

Pinch salt

2 tablespoons cornstarch

3 tablespoons plus 1 teaspoon granulated sugar

1 tablespoon water

1 Preheat the oven to 400°F. On a lightly floured work surface, roll the dough into an 11-inch circle and place it on a nonstick baking sheet. Spread ¼ cup of the preserves on top of the crust, leaving a 2-inch border. Set aside.

2 In a large bowl, combine the pears, lemon juice, raisins, if using, brown sugar, cinnamon, nutmeg, and salt. In a small bowl, combine the cornstarch with 3 tablespoons of the granulated sugar. Mix well. Sprinkle over the pear mixture and toss well to coat.

3 Arrange the pear mixture on top of the preserves, leaving a 2-inch border. Fold the edges of dough over the pears toward the center, pressing gently to seal (the dough will only partially cover the fruit). Sprinkle the remaining 1 teaspoon granulated sugar over the fruit mixture. Bake until the crust is lightly browned, 30 to 40 minutes. Allow to cool on a wire rack.

4 In a small saucepan, heat the remaining 2 tablespoons preserves and the water over medium heat until it is smooth and melted, about 2 minutes. Brush the glaze on the exposed pears. Serve warm or at room temperature.

Mixed Fruit Cobbler

<50¢ per serving

Makes 8 servings

Use this recipe as a pattern to make a cobbler using one or more of your favorite fruits, from apples to berries. This version uses both fresh and canned fruit, but you can use whatever is on hand, ripe, or in season, to equal a total of 4 to 5 cups of fruit filling.

4 medium ripe peaches, peeled, halved, pitted, and chopped

3 medium ripe plums, peeled, halved, pitted, and chopped

1 (15-ounce) can pineapple chunks, drained, reserving ⅔ cup juice

1½ cups all-purpose flour

½ cup sugar

1½ teaspoons baking powder

½ teaspoon salt

⅓ cup vegan margarine, melted

1 teaspoon pure vanilla extract

❶ Preheat the oven to 350°F. Grease a 9-inch square baking pan. Combine the peaches, plums, and pineapple in the bottom of the prepared pan and set aside.

❷ In a medium bowl, combine the flour, sugar, baking powder, and salt. Stir in the pineapple juice, margarine, and vanilla and mix until well blended.

❸ Drop the dough onto the filling with a large spoon to cover, but do not spread it out (it can be uneven: rustic is good). Bake until golden and bubbling, about 50 minutes. Serve warm.

Splurge a Little

Serve à la mode with vegan vanilla ice cream.

Chocolate-Blueberry Crumble

<50¢
per serving

Makes 8 servings

The combination of blueberries and chocolate may sound unusual, but wait until you taste this easy dessert. It's most economical when fresh blueberries are in season or frozen ones are on sale.

2 cups fresh or thawed frozen blueberries	Grated zest of 1 lemon
½ cup vegan semisweet chocolate chips	¾ cup all-purpose flour
½ cup plus 2 tablespoons sugar	½ cup quick-cooking oats
	¾ cup vegan margarine, melted
	2 teaspoons ground cinnamon

1 Preheat the oven to 350°F. In a large bowl, combine the blueberries, chocolate chips, 2 tablespoons of the sugar, and zest, mixing well. Spread the mixture evenly into a 9-inch pie plate. Set aside

2 In a medium bowl, combine the flour, oats, remaining ½ cup sugar, margarine, and cinnamon. Mix until crumbly.

3 Sprinkle the mixture evenly on top of the blueberries. Bake until the top is lightly browned, about 25 minutes. Cool on a wire rack at least 15 minutes before serving. Serve warm spooned into bowls.

Tropical Betty

Makes 8 servings

This old-fashioned dessert known as a Betty differs from a crisp in its use of bread crumbs. It's typically made with apples, but I like to mix it up with what's on hand. In this version, Betty goes tropical with ripe bananas, canned pineapple, and coconut (although you could add other tropical fruit if you have some on hand). Like most desserts of this type, it tastes best served warm topped with vegan vanilla ice cream.

1 (13-ounce) can unsweetened coconut milk

½ cup plain unsweetened or vanilla soy milk

1 (15-ounce) can crushed pineapple, drained, reserving ½ cup juice

2 ripe bananas, cut into ½-inch slices

1 teaspoon pure vanilla extract

1 teaspoon coconut extract

4 cups fresh bread crumbs (see Note)

¼ cup vegan margarine, melted

⅔ cup packed dark brown sugar

2 teaspoons ground cinnamon

3 tablespoons unsweetened shredded coconut

❶ Preheat the oven to 350°F. Lightly oil an 8-inch square baking pan and set aside.

❷ In a medium saucepan, combine the coconut milk, soy milk, and pineapple juice. Bring to a boil, then remove from heat and set aside to cool. Spread the pineapple and bananas in the bottom of the prepared pan. Stir the vanilla and the coconut extract into the cooled coconut milk mixture.

❸ In a large bowl, combine the bread crumbs, margarine, sugar, and cinnamon. Mix well. Pour the coconut milk mixture over the crumb mixture, pressing with the back of a spoon to immerse the crumbs in the liquid. Set aside for 10 minutes.

❹ Spread the soaked crumb mixture over the fruit. Bake until set and nicely browned on top, about 45 minutes. About 30 minutes into baking, sprinkle the coconut on top. Cool on a wire rack for 30 minutes before serving.

Note: *To make fresh bread crumbs:* Tear 2 slices of Italian bread and put in a food processor. Pulse until the bread pieces become a bit smaller, then process for a few seconds to make coarse crumbs. Remove the crumbs and repeat with as much bread as needed to make 4 cups for this recipe. Store any remaining crumbs in an airtight container for another use. The crumbs will keep at room temperature for a few days or can be frozen for a month or two.

Splurge a Little

Add chopped fresh mango to replace some of the pineapple and banana. Sprinkle 2 tablespoons crushed macadamia nuts or cashews on top when you add the shredded coconut.

Chocolate-Cherry Bread Pudding

<$1.00 per serving

Makes 6 servings

Chocolate and cherries are a great combination, but fresh cherries are expensive. One solution is this luscious bread pudding that uses cherry fruit spread and dried cherries. Because it's easy to make and it makes a lot, this is a good choice when you have to make dessert for a crowd.

1 loaf Italian bread, cut into ½-inch slices, crusts removed

½ cup dried cherries

⅔ cup sugar

3 cups plain unsweetened or vanilla soy milk

1 (12-ounce) bag vegan semisweet chocolate chips

2 cups firm tofu, drained and crumbled

1 teaspoon pure vanilla extract

1 cup cherry preserves

1 teaspoon fresh lemon juice

❶ Grease a 9 × 13-inch baking pan. Cut the bread into cubes (you should have 6 to 8 cups) and arrange them evenly in the bottom of the prepared pan. Sprinkle evenly with the cherries and set aside.

❷ In a large saucepan, combine the sugar and soy milk and bring just to a boil. Remove from heat and add the chocolate chips, stirring until the chocolate is melted. Set aside.

❸ Place the tofu and vanilla in a blender or food processor. Add about ½ cup of the chocolate mixture and blend until smooth, then add the remaining chocolate mixture and blend until smooth and creamy.

❹ Pour the chocolate mixture evenly over the bread cubes, covering all the bread. Press down on the bread with back of a spoon to make sure all the bread is covered with the chocolate mixture. Set aside.

❺ In a small bowl, combine the preserves and the lemon juice and stir until smooth. Drizzle the cherry mixture over the bread pudding, poking some of it down into the bread mixture to distribute evenly. Cover with foil and set aside for 30 minutes at room temperature. Preheat the oven to 350°F. Bake covered until just set, about 1 hour. Let cool for 10 minutes before serving.

Substitute 1 cup of pitted fresh cherries for the dried, or garnish each serving with a few fresh cherries. Top with vegan whipped cream or vegan vanilla ice cream.

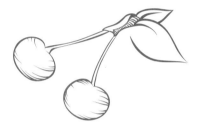

Cheap Thrills

When you need a quick and easy dessert and there's no time to bake, think "fire and ice." Make a special dessert by scooping vegan ice cream into pretty dessert bowls. Then, melt some vegan margarine and a little light brown sugar in a skillet, add your choice of sliced fruit (bananas, pineapple, apples, peaches are all good) and some nuts, if you like. Finish with a splash of rum, brandy, or your favorite liqueur (or not). Spoon the warmed fruit mixture over the ice cream and you have a delicious dessert special enough for company. It's a great way to stretch a pint of vegan ice cream to keep the cost in check.

Tiramisù Bread Pudding

<$1.00 per serving

Makes 6 servings

Italian bread is used to replace the cake in this version of the classic Italian dessert, and coffee-laced cashew cream stands in for the mascarpone cheese, resulting in a delicious, healthful, and thrifty dessert.

4 (1-inch-thick) slices Italian bread, crusts removed

⅓ cup vanilla soy milk

¾ cup sugar

2 tablespoons brandy or dark rum (optional)

1 tablespoon plus 1 teaspoon unsweetened cocoa powder

¾ cup unsalted raw cashews

⅓ cup strong brewed coffee, cooled to room temperature

1 teaspoon pure vanilla extract

1 (10.5-ounce) package firm silken tofu, drained and patted dry

Vegan chocolate curls, for garnish (optional)

1 Grease an 8-inch square baking pan. Cut the bread slices into 1-inch cubes arrange them evenly in the bottom of the pan. Set aside.

2 In a small saucepan, heat the soy milk and ¼ cup of the sugar just to a boil. Remove from the heat and stir in the brandy, if using. Pour the soy milk mixture over the bread, piercing the bread with a fork to help the mixture soak in. Sprinkle with 1 teaspoon of the cocoa and set aside.

3 In a high-speed blender, grind the cashews to a powder. Add the coffee, vanilla, and remaining ½ cup sugar and blend until smooth. Add the tofu and blend until smooth and creamy. Spread the mixture evenly across the bread layer in the pan. Sprinkle with the remaining 1 tablespoon cocoa. Refrigerate for at least 2 hours before serving. When ready to serve, garnish with chocolate curls, if using.

Chocolate Chip– Walnut Rice Pudding

<$1.00 per serving

Makes 4 servings

In this recipe, the usually straitlaced rice pudding gets all glitzed up with chocolate chips and walnuts for a yummy new take on an old-fashioned favorite. Although many people think of rice pudding as an all-American dessert, it's actually popular throughout the world, from Scandinavia to Asia. And why not? It's wholesome, economical, and delicious. Use any kind of non-dairy milk you prefer, from soy or rice to almond or coconut, and whatever long-grain or quick-cooking rice you have on hand. Fragrant basmati or jasmine are especially good, although jasmine will take less time to cook, about 20 minutes. For a more traditional version, omit the chocolate chips and walnuts, and add a teaspoon of cinnamon and ½ cup of raisins.

½ cup long-grain rice

3 cups plain unsweetened or vanilla soy milk or other nondairy milk

Pinch salt

½ cup sugar

⅓ cup chopped walnuts

1½ teaspoons pure vanilla extract

½ cup vegan semisweet chocolate chips

1 In a large saucepan, combine the rice, soy milk, and salt and bring to a boil over high heat. Reduce the heat to medium and simmer, stirring frequently, until the rice is soft, about 30 minutes.

2 Stir in the sugar and continue to cook for 5 minutes or until the sugar is dissolved and the pudding has thickened. Remove from heat, stir in the walnuts and the vanilla, and set aside to cool.

3 When the pudding is cooled, stir in the chocolate chips. Spoon the pudding into dessert bowls, then cover and refrigerate for 1 hour or longer before serving.

Caramel Baked Apples

Makes 4 to 8 servings

This home-style dessert is basically baked apples stuffed with bread pudding and topped with a luscious caramel sauce. A scoop of vegan vanilla ice cream makes a great addition, in which case you may want to serve only one stuffed apple half per person instead of two.

Apples

2 cups fresh bread crumbs
(see page 235)
¼ cup finely chopped walnut pieces
⅓ cup light brown sugar
1½ teaspoons ground cinnamon
1 tablespoon vegan margarine,
melted
¼ cup apple juice or plain
unsweetened or vanilla soy milk
4 large Granny Smith apples

Sauce

½ cup light brown sugar
¼ cup vegan margarine
⅓ cup plain unsweetened or vanilla
soy milk
4½ teaspoons pure maple syrup
½ teaspoon pure vanilla extract

1 Make the apples: In a large bowl, combine the bread crumbs, walnuts, sugar, cinnamon, margarine, and apple juice. Stir until well blended. Set aside.

2 Grease a 9-inch square baking pan and set aside. Halve and core the apples. Spoon an equal amount of the bread mixture onto each apple half and use your fingers to press the mixture firmly into each apple. Arrange the apples, stuffed side up, in the prepared pan. Set aside. Preheat the oven to 350°F.

3 Make the sauce: In a medium saucepan, heat the sugar and margarine over medium heat, stirring until the sugar is dissolved and the margarine is melted. Stir in the soy milk and maple syrup and bring just to a boil. Remove from heat and stir in the vanilla.

4 Spoon about half of the sauce mixture over the apples and set the remaining sauce aside. Cover the pan tightly with foil and bake until the apples are tender, about 40 minutes or longer, depending on the size of the apples.

5 To serve, arrange 1 or 2 apple halves in a shallow dessert bowl and drizzle with some of the remaining sauce.

Vegan Whipped Cream

< 50¢
per serving

Makes about 2 cups

2 tablespoons vegan margarine

½ cup sugar

1 tablespoon plain unsweetened or
    vanilla soy milk

2 teaspoons pure vanilla extract

1 (10.5-ounce) package firm
    silken tofu, drained and
    blotted dry

❶ In a small saucepan, melt the margarine over medium heat. Add the sugar and soy milk and cook over low heat, stirring until the sugar dissolves. Remove from the heat and stir in the vanilla.

❷ Combine the sugar mixture and the tofu in a blender and blend until very smooth and creamy. Transfer to a bowl, cover, and refrigerate until chilled. This tastes best if used on the same day that it is made.

Splurge a Little

Buy ready-made vegan whipped cream at a natural food store.

Online Resources

Whether you are interested in locating a CSA or u-pick farm or finding super-market coupons and other deals on vegan products, here are some online sources that can help.

Community Supported Agriculture

Local Harvest
www.localharvest.org
This searchable website allows you to find local CSA farms throughout the country.

EatWell Guide
www.eatwellguide.org
A directory of family farms, restaurants, food co-ops, farmers markets and other purveyors of local organic foods.

Biodynamic Farming and Gardening Association
www.biodynamics.com
Information on biodynamic principles, methods, and techniques that promote the growth of quality produce.

U-Pick Produce

Pick Your Own
www.pickyourown.org
This website allows you to search for local u-pick farms throughout the country to find hours, directions, and what's available for

picking. It also provides useful information such as tips for canning and freezing.

Vegan Product Retailers

In addition to checking your local natural food stores and food co-ops for sales and discounts, visit these online vegan retailers. They sometimes offer coupons or special sales prices on many of the products they sell.

Vegan Essentials
www.veganessentials.com
Carries a wide range of vegan lifestyle items, including food products.

Food Fight Vegan Grocery
www.foodfightgrocery.com
Offers vegan food items and lifestyle products.

Cosmo's Vegan Shoppe
www.cosmosveganshoppe.com
A source for vegan groceries and lifestyle goods.

Pangea
www.veganstore.com
Sells vegan ingredients and other vegan goods.

Mail Order Catalog for Healthy Eating
www.healthy-eating.com
Carries vegan food products and lifestyle items.

Grocery Coupon Websites

A number of general grocery coupon websites offer printable coupons for general supermarket items. If you're a coupon clipper, these sites are worth a look to search for products that you use.

www.grocerycoupons.com

www.ppgazette.com

www.retailmenot.com

Other Sources

Company Websites

If you like particular vegan products, it's worth checking the individual company websites for money-saving coupons.

Supermarket Websites

Visit the websites of specific supermarkets in your area for local online store coupons and sale information.

Caring Consumer

www.caringconsumer.com/coupons.asp.

This "guide to kinder living" site contains product information with links to product coupons for money-saving bargains (many are non-grocery items, but they include vegan personal care and pet products.)

Index

C